In a Nutshell

Dialogues
with Parents at Acorn Hill
A Waldorf Kindergarten

Nancy Foster

Published 2005 by
Acorn Hill Waldorf Kindergarten & Nursery
9504 Brunett Avenue
Silver Spring, MD 20901
301.565.2282
www.acornhill.org

Book design and illustration by
Sheila Harrington, Studio Five, Washington, DC

Printed in the United States of America

Books can be ordered from
Waldorf Early Childhood Association
285 Hungry Hollow Road
Spring Valley, New York 10977
845.352.1690
or visit the online bookstore at
http://www.waldorfearlychildhood.org

Table of Contents

Foreword i

Preface iii

Introduction v

Our Classroom Environment

Color in the Classroom 3

Why Curtains? 5

Teachers' Dress 7

The Significance of Candles 9

Naming the Teacher 11

No Cars and Trucks? 13

What About Puzzles? 15

Musical Instruments in the Classroom 17

Work and Play at School

The Rhythm of the Morning 23

Saying "You may…" 25

Ironing in the Classroom: Danger? 27

Boys and Waldorf Education 29

Playing Cats and Dogs 33

Music in the Mood of the Fifth 37

Can Energetic Boys Enjoy Handwork? 39

Gun Play at School 41

Field Trips?..45

Fairy Tales for Young Children 47

The Challenge of Circle Time 49

Puppetry and "Told" Stories 51

Children at Home

Colors for a Child's Bedroom 55

Older and Younger Siblings...57

Boredom 61

Telephone..65

Bedtime Ritual 67

Feeding a Child..69

Swords vs. Guns 71

TV Away from Home...73

Barbie 75

Forbidden Words?..77

Appropriate Gifts 79

"What did you learn in school today?" 81

Toys in the Neighborhood 83

Helping Children in a Time of Trouble—A Few Thoughts.....85

Is the World a Good Place? 87

In Conclusion..91

About the Author 93

Foreword

Written by kindergarten teacher Nancy Foster for parents at Acorn Hill Waldorf Kindergarten and Nursery, this collection of "Question and Answer" articles from the Acorn Hill *In a Nutshell* provides a wonderful, practical resource for parents and teachers of young children. We can all benefit from reading Nancy's insights and advice, developed over many years of working with young children and their parents.

These reflections are glimpses into the intimate dialogue between parent and teacher. They are a record of one teacher's attempt to share with parents that which lies behind the outer activities of their child's kindergarten experience. These offerings do not claim to be the only or definitive answer to the questions asked, or the "one right way." Each Waldorf kindergarten is unique, and other Waldorf early childhood educators might offer quite different answers to many of these questions.

In fact, if there are so many different approaches, then we might ask, what is it that makes a Waldorf kindergarten "Waldorf?" This collection of answers provides an insight into this question: this unique "Waldorf" element has to do with the particular kind of conscious love and care each teacher offers toward every aspect of the young child's experience. Ultimately, Waldorf early childhood education is not a "program," but an art.

We thank Nancy Foster and Acorn Hill for sharing these wonderful seed thoughts from *In a Nutshell* with a wider audience; and we hope that they will stimulate fruitful dialogue among parents and early childhood educators in our wider community.

Susan Howard
Coordinator
Waldorf Early Childhood Association of North America

Preface

I am the parent of two daughters, now fine young women, both of whom attended Acorn Hill when they were small. Being a parent has been a joy, a blessing, and, often, a challenge. I remember in particular a time when my older daughter Sarah was six years old. She had reverted, I felt, to two-year-old behavior, defiant, prone to tantrums, and full of the word "NO!" She had me stumped, and I needed advice. So I found myself on the phone with Nancy Foster, who was her kindergarten teacher at the time. Nancy, after listening to my frustration and concern, began simply, "And what did you do when she was two?" Light dawned! I mentioned several ideas, and then Nancy made a few suggestions and encouraged me to see what would happen. The details are now lost to my memory, but what remains is my appreciation for her thoughtful response, the fact that her advice worked, and how I felt both respected and valued as a parent, and supported by her insight.

Parents in Waldorf schools can learn much from their child's teacher, both about Waldorf education and creative parenting. Waldorf teachers can also provide a warm sense of caring and support. Such was my experience with Nancy. Because Waldorf education brings an approach to the kindergarten classroom that differs from traditional and progressive early childhood pedagogy, parents have questions, and many are perennial: Why are our kindergartens painted pink? Why do Acorn Hill teachers still wear dresses? Where are the puzzles? The Waldorf approach also offers much in the way of family life and parenting. Parents frequently ask: What about gun play? Barbie dolls? Television?

Nancy took these questions and more, and created a venue for them in a column in our monthly newsletter, *In a Nutshell*. Nancy has taught at Acorn Hill for more than 30 years. She is our own "authority" on Waldorf education, child development and parenting. "Ask Nancy" is heard frequently from faculty and parents alike, and is the nickname parents have given to her monthly column. Nancy offers lucid, thoughtful and personal answers. When she gives advice, it is always with the encouragement to think about it, to try it, but with the recognition that the parent must decide what works best. She is sometimes provocative, but is also respect-ful of the parent's point of view.

As a parent in Nancy's class, I greatly appreciated her clear and thoughtful advice and insight about my child. As the administrator at Acorn Hill, it has been a joy and privilege to direct new parents to "ask Nancy" with their own questions about Waldorf education and parenting. I hope our Acorn Hill community will enjoy this collection of Nancy's columns, and that parents elsewhere will find it just as helpful. And if you find yourself with a new question, let us know, and we will continue to "ask Nancy."

Janet Johnson
Administrator
Acorn Hill Waldorf Kindergarten and Nursery

Introduction

These dialogues-in-print are based on a "Question and Answer"
column from *In a Nutshell*, the newsletter of our school, Acorn Hill
Waldorf Kindergarten and Nursery. As Pedagogical Chair, former Waldorf
parent, and long-time teacher at Acorn Hill, first in the mixed-age kindergarten and then in nursery and parent/child groups, it was my privilege to
offer answers to questions submitted by parents.

For some parents, the first impressions of a Waldorf school bring the
feeling, "Yes! This is just what we've been looking for, not only for our
child, but for ourselves." For others, there may be a sense of, "Hm-m-m,
this is quite interesting. Let's try it and see how it goes." Whatever the first
impressions, however, it seems that many parents feel at one time or another as if they have stumbled upon an alien culture, with practices which
appear unusual or strange. Questions may arise about their children's
experiences at school and about the Waldorf approach to early childhood
education.

Our faculty learned that parents were sometimes hesitant to ask these
questions. Perhaps they didn't want to bother their child's busy teacher, or
they were afraid their question might offend; sometimes they were not sure
how to put their question into words, feeling that they might not have a
grasp of the "Waldorf vocabulary." We therefore decided to offer this opportunity for parents to present questions anonymously, if they wished.

The "Question and Answer" column became a regular feature in the
newsletter, and questions ranged far and wide. It was always interesting to
see what concerns might arise. The original idea for the column was that
questions would relate specifically to Acorn Hill and Waldorf education.
As time passed, however, many questions were asked about life at home
with young children. These were welcome, as well.

This book's title refers, of course, to the name of our school newsletter.
It also, however, hints at the nature of the question-and-answer format:
short answers to sometimes complex questions. In almost every case, much
more could be said. The answers are also in an informal style, composed
almost as if I were writing a letter to a friend.

Of course, any particular teacher might answer these questions somewhat differently. All of us base our work on continuing study of Anthroposophy. Rudolf Steiner's insights into the nature and development of the human being are the foundation of Waldorf education. The individual teacher's understanding and creativity also play an essential role, however. The answers I offer, therefore, should be taken as thoughts-in-process, as a stimulus for the reader's own thinking and further inquiry, not as "the correct answer."

For this publication, the questions have been grouped in three sections: "Our Classroom Environment," "Work and Play at School," and "Children at Home." Beyond that, the questions in each group appear roughly in the order of their original publication, with no intention to organize them by topic. I hope readers will feel free to browse, and to pick and choose as fancy strikes or need arises.

Finally, I offer heartfelt thanks to the parents and children who have been, and continue to be, my most valuable teachers. It is a great joy to know them and share their experiences. Thanks also to my colleagues for their support, and in particular to our Administrator, Janet Johnson, who has done the essential work of overseeing production of this book. I am grateful to friend and former colleague Mary Rein, who contributed her skill as a proofreader in addition to warm encouragement. For the cover art, as well as design and layout of the book, I thank graphic designer/ illustrator Sheila Harrington, who also happens to be an Acorn Hill parent. Her professional expertise and artistic sensitivity were of great benefit to our project and its outcome.

Nancy Foster
Acorn Hill Waldorf Kindergarten and Nursery
May 2005

Our Classroom Environment

Color in the Classroom

Question

Why are the classrooms at Acorn Hill so monochromatic? I am accustomed to seeing more patterns and designs on fabrics and surfaces. All this pinkness, and the solid pastel colors, seem strange to me.

Answer

The environment at Acorn Hill is intended to meet the needs of the young child, as we understand those needs. This is true on the level of physical equipment—low tables, small chairs, play materials which encourage imagination and invite the use of large and small muscles. It is also true on the level of the sensory surroundings. We feel that solid colors in warm, light-filled hues best protect and nourish the child's delicate, still-developing senses, allowing the eyes to rest peacefully rather than overstimulating them with bright or "busy" patterns. The soft rose or peach colors of the walls are intended to create that sense of young life which one feels in an orchard of fruit trees in bloom.

The soft, plain wall colors could be compared to the faces of the simple dolls in our classrooms. These faces do not impose themselves on the children by way of a set expression, but allow the children to bring their own particular inner needs into play. The wall colors, likewise, are quiet enough to allow the children a certain inner freedom. The simplicity of the color scheme also allows the soft forms and colors of the wool pictures on the wall to shine forth in their gentle way—full of movement and depth, yet leaving much to the viewer's imagination.

Strong, bright colors, however, are also welcome at times, and may be especially sought out by particular children. For this reason, we provide play cloths or capes in a variety of colors and shades. In our classroom, for example, the colors include red, deep green, purple, deep blue, and a mottled brown, in addition to lighter colors. Our dolls and puppets also come in an array of colors.

Many people are personally or culturally attuned more to patterns than to solid colors, or to intense colors rather than pastels, and for them our environment may create a sense almost of disorientation or "culture shock." I have not forgotten my own initial reaction to the pink walls when I first entered a Waldorf kindergarten. Once I understood that the same care had gone into the choice of color as into the rest of the program and environment which seemed so right and so health-bringing for the young child, I was able to become accustomed to the colors and to appreciate them. In today's world of fast-moving life and sensory overstimulation, it seems particularly important to create a space in which children are free to create their own inner colors and patterns. 🌿

Why Curtains?

Question

Why do you have curtains in your classroom windows? The woods outside are beautiful, and with your emphasis on the seasons, it seems that you would want the children to be able to observe the world of nature through the windows.

Answer

You may have heard us compare the child's experience of the morning at school to the rhythm of breathing, which is essentially an alternation of contraction (breathing in) and expansion (breathing out), a rhythm basic to all of life. The group expands (breathes out) in creative play time, for example, and contracts (breathes in) at circle time. This rhythm creates a sense of well-being in the young child, since it follows a natural process and does not keep the child too long at either end of the spectrum. It also helps the child to become a socialized human being, learning that there is a time and place for everything (well, perhaps not everything. . . !).

The breathing rhythm—contraction and expansion—can also be created in the child's surroundings. Its application to architectural design is a topic too large to address here, but you can perhaps understand how it relates to the use of curtains. When the children are indoors, we want to give them the sense of being "held" or nurtured by the space they occupy. They feel secure, cozy, and inwardly warm, able to give themselves up to their play, or to singing or listening to a story. The opposite extreme might be a gym, with its large space and high ceiling; many small children feel either intimidated or overstimulated in such an environment.

Our curtains, then, help to create the inward pole of the children's experience, so that they are not distracted or drawn outward by what is happening outdoors. When they do go outdoors for play time, they "expand" or breathe out into the natural environment with a wonderful sense of satisfaction. As you can see, the children are experiencing a breathing rhythm in space as well as a breathing rhythm in time—both wonderfully health-giving.

Teachers' Dress

Question

Why do Acorn Hill teachers always wear skirts or dresses? Is there a dress code you follow as to colors, etc.? If so, why?

Answer

As you know, Waldorf early childhood teachers try to create an environment of beauty, simplicity, and order for the young child, knowing that this is an important aspect of nourishing their senses, avoiding overstimulation, and laying the basis for healthy physical, emotional, and intellectual development. We also seek to provide an atmosphere of nurturing warmth and security. The teacher is, in a sense, part of the environment and atmosphere.

We feel that a dress or skirt gives an impression of fullness and softness. This can convey to a child a sense of warmth and protection, as in the old-time image of a small child peeking out from the safe haven of Mother's skirts. One kindergarten teacher has found that a very young child who is having difficulty at circle time can be brought along by being invited to hold on to the teacher's skirt. This is obviously not to say that someone wearing pants cannot offer love and security to a child. In our clothing, however, we are trying not only to offer that warmth, but to bring the image as well.

Wearing a skirt or dress also presents a simplified impression of the human form; as one perceptive parent observed, this is the same effect given by our standing dolls (table puppets). A full, soft skirt does not emphasize the human anatomy, but rather presents the archetypal form of human uprightness. Of course a very long, full skirt could hamper movement—as would a tight skirt, but in a different way. Practical considerations certainly enter in. Likewise, there might be occasions when pants are more appropriate: on work days, for example, or if the teacher is sledding with the children.

And what if the kindergarten teacher is a man? We actually had occasion to consult on this matter with a father of four who is an experienced Waldorf kindergarten teacher. He said that he wears fairly loose-fitting trousers (as opposed to tight jeans), and he wears an apron which he feels helps to give some of that warmth and fullness which nourish the children. Almost all Waldorf kindergarten teachers wear aprons for at least part of the morning, as do the parents in our Parent/Child groups, as a practical matter—to protect our clothing—as well as to reflect the fact that we are busying ourselves taking care of the life of the "family:" baking, washing, ironing, caring for the room, making festival preparations, taking part in artistic activity, and so forth. In other words, we are here to carry out our daily tasks in the company of the children, whether they are working with us or playing (their own particular version of "work").

As to color, we generally try to wear solid colors, since these are more restful to the eye and do not assert themselves in the environment as more active patterns do. We also tend to wear soft colors, so as to leave the children inwardly free. Some children feel comfortable with delicate colors; others are drawn to stronger, brighter shades. We try to make sure that these needs may be satisfied by providing play cloths and capes in a variety of colors and shades.

In general, we try to dress with simplicity, in a way that does not call attention to personality or style. This is our school "persona;" in other environments we may dress quite differently. But for the children, we are "Teacher" in the way that a parent is "Mommy" or "Daddy," and often they scarcely realize that we have any existence beyond the school. Numerous comments have shown us that many of the younger children assume we sleep at school. A three-year-old recently noted with some concern that the basket bed in our room is awfully small. Presumably he was wondering how my assistant and I managed to be comfortable there at night! If younger children see a teacher in some other setting, such as the market, they are often visibly confused. A sense of the teacher as a "real person" with a separate life only seems to dawn around age six or so; in fact, for me a sign of first-grade readiness has been the child's asking me questions about my personal life. We do not want to infringe on the younger child's assumption that we are here totally for him or her.

Our choice of clothing is not the result of a dress code, but rather is part of our effort to honor the nature and needs of the children in our care.

The Significance of Candles

Question

Why are candles used in the classroom?

Answer

There are several reasons. Candles can help to create a mood of quiet and wonder at circle time or story time. Some parents like to light a candle for their child's bedtime ritual, for this reason. Candles can lend a festive air to special occasions such as a classroom festival or birthday observance. In the Waldorf kindergarten we try to help children to experience all four of the traditional elements: earth, water, air, and fire. Thus the candle flame plays a role in this connection. An important lesson for the children is the need to treat fire with care and respect in order to enjoy its light and warmth in safety; the children absorb this lesson through the way the teacher cares for the lighted candle.

Perhaps most important of all, the candle can be seen as a picture of the spirit-light within each human being, and of the transformation of matter into spirit, as the beeswax (preferable to paraffin) is changed into light. This is a potent symbol, and though unspoken, the teacher's awareness of this presence of the spirit can help to nurture the child's natural sense of reverence and wonder.

In order to keep the lighting of the candle a special, wonder-filled experience, I light a candle in my classroom only once a day, for the morning verse at circle time. Other teachers may light one at story time instead, or at both times. We like to snuff the candle rather than blow it out, because this brings more of a sense of care and appreciation for the light we have been given.

Naming the Teacher

Question

Why are some teachers addressed as Mrs. [last name], while others are called Miss [first name]? Is this confusing for the children when they move from one class to another?

Answer

Some teachers were brought up to call adults by Mr. or Mrs., and they feel most comfortable with this practice for the children in their classes. It seems to them to encourage a healthy sense of respect in children.

Other Acorn Hill teachers, however, prefer to be addressed as "Miss [Jane]," and in some Waldorf kindergartens, both in the U.S. and abroad, teachers are called by the first name alone. These teachers feel that using last names is better saved for children in the grades, when the teacher is seen more as an authority, whereas in the kindergarten the teacher should be more a motherly (or fatherly) figure. This is a matter which seems to depend a great deal on the customs of a particular school or region, as well as the particular teacher's feeling of what is comfortable and appropriate.

It often happens, especially with the younger children, that the teacher is addressed simply as "Teacher." This is a bit like calling a parent "Mommy" or "Daddy," in that it designates the person's role in relation to the child. We teachers often notice that children do not regard us as individuals with a life apart from them and the school; we simply are "Teacher." It is not until they approach the end of the kindergarten years that many children become aware that the teacher does exist as a person with a life of her own. It is important to honor these different perceptions, allowing the children to awaken in their own good time.

In any case, children do not seem at all confused or disturbed by the different designations chosen by different teachers. They seem simply to accept the name as it is. In fact, I suspect that most of them have little, if any, awareness of the difference, much less of any significance it may have. Perhaps it is more of an issue for the adults than for the children.

No Cars and Trucks?

Question

How do you choose toys and play materials for the classrooms? I understand that you try to have non-specific, open-ended equipment, but why do you provide play dishes and pots and pans, but no cars or trucks?

Answer

As you said, we wish to provide play materials which support and stimulate the young child's capacity for fantasy play—the ability to use objects in many different ways to meet the needs of the moment. A carved piece of wood may, for example, be used as a bridge, or as a telephone, a boat, a cradle, a delivery truck, a fish, merchandise for a store, a package for the mailman to deliver, etc. etc. Younger children, of course, may see it as just another piece of "firewood" for the "fires" they love to build by piling up every moveable object in the room. The wooden plates and bowls, likewise, can serve a variety of purposes, and at the end of playtime can sometimes be found in the drawstring bags where they have been stashed as treasure, or mail, or just something to carry around. To be sure, they are often used for setting the table or for playing restaurant and cooking a variety of dishes, from pizza to apple pie, and sometimes "poison!" Both boys and girls enjoy these uses.

Cars and trucks, however, are more specific in orientation, because they have wheels. In theory, they could be used for many of the same purposes named above for the carved piece of wood. The wheels, however, seem to speak so strongly of locomotion—particularly fast locomotion—that these vehicles are rarely used for other purposes. When I first began teaching at Acorn Hill, we did have simple wooden cars and trucks in the classroom. Our experience showed, however, that these were used almost exclusively by the boys. Furthermore, these toys were not used constructively; rather, the play invariably degenerated into zooming them around and crashing them into each other. My own sons had cars and trucks at home; they loved playing with them and made many elaborate set-ups with them, playing quite constructively and even, at times, imaginatively. Somehow in the group situation, however, this seemed impossible.

Eventually, therefore, we eliminated these vehicles from the classroom. The large stumps and playstands often become trucks, buses, trains, or airplanes, and are much better suited to creative play, since the children can actually ride in them and take "journeys," rather than pushing them around wildly on the floor. 🌿

What About Puzzles?

Question

Why are there no puzzles in the classrooms at Acorn Hill?

Answer

In equipping a Waldorf nursery or kindergarten classroom, we are mindful that our purpose is not to entertain children or "keep them busy," but to help them find their way into real life in the most healthy, joyful way possible. Thus, we hope that the play materials we provide will help to nurture and develop qualities such as enthusiasm, curiosity, reverence for life, self-direction, creativity, flexible thinking, respect for others. . .

Puzzles may be entertaining for some children. However, it can be said that the whole point of a puzzle is to find the correct placement for each puzzle piece. This is the case whether it is a very simple puzzle with single set-in pieces, or a complex jigsaw puzzle for adults. Through its very essence, the puzzle teaches the child that there is just one "right way" to see something. This is the antithesis of flexible thinking, in which it is necessary—and enlivening—to see things from different viewpoints. We prefer to provide the children with more open-ended playthings, which can be maneuvered and placed in a variety of ways according to the needs of the situation or the child's changing fantasy.

In addition, it is good for the young child, who is still learning about the world and the objects and beings which inhabit it, to see the wholeness of things. In many puzzles, objects (animals, people, trees, etc.) are arbitrarily divided into pieces in a way that does not reflect reality or function. This surely cannot be a positive support to a child's experience.

There do exist some "Waldorf-style" puzzles, which are beautiful, with lovely forms and colors. Nevertheless, these embody the same "one right way" approach and, we feel, should be avoided in the pre-school years.

Musical Instruments in the Classroom

Question

Could you address the question of musical instruments in the class-room? I notice that the lyre is the only instrument used by the teacher. Wouldn't it be good for the children to have a broader experience? And what about rhythm instruments for the children? Many preschools have these available, and I haven't seen this at Acorn Hill.

Answer

The young child's sense of hearing, like the other senses, is still delicate and impressionable, and it is our responsibility both to protect and to nurture this very important sense, which is one of the young child's gateways to the world.

In a subtle way, we learn something about the quality, the essence, of whatever substance is producing a sound. Have you ever tapped a bowl with your fingernail in an effort to determine whether it is made of porcelain, or look-alike plastic, or glass? This is just one example of what our hearing can tell us.

In bringing an infant into the world, we want most of all to welcome him or her into the realm of human beings—into the family, and then gradually into the wider world of friends and community. Thus it follows that at first the most important sounds are human sounds: gentle speaking, and singing. The human voice could be said to be the first musical instrument, and for the early years of life it remains the most important instrument for the child both to hear and to "play." How fortunate is the child whose parents sing at home. Never mind if the voice is not beautiful; because it expresses the inner qualities of love and warmth, it is a great gift to the child. In the Waldorf early childhood classroom, we use the voice with care and love, and singing is heard often during the morning.

Another important "musical instrument" is the human body. At circle time we may clap, pat our legs, stamp our feet, or drum our fingertips on the floor to create sounds. Older children love to practice snapping their fingers, listening closely for that certain sound. During playtime children can often be seen and heard creating sounds with the objects around them—tapping or pounding stones together, or beating a stump with a stick. They may also use play materials as imaginary instruments; one boy in my class frequently sought out a particular curved length of wood which he liked to use as a saxophone. This always gave him great satisfaction—and the rest of us did not have to endure the actual sound of a saxophone at close quarters!

Because we prefer to offer the children open-ended play materials— that is, materials which can be used in many different ways, according to the child's needs of the moment—we also do not provide many of the traditional rhythm toys. However, some teachers do have bells, gourds, or perhaps a drum or pentatonic xylophone available in the classroom. These allow the children further opportunities to explore sound. It is important that these instruments produce a good quality sound and, in the case of the xylophone, that the notes are in tune. The children may play freely with these instruments, as long as they treat them with appropriate care and the sounds do not become disruptive to the mood of the classroom. In these early years, the children are not asked to play these instruments in a particular rhythm, and in my class I do not use rhythm instruments during circle time, since I feel it is better for the children to find their own way into the world of rhythm rather than having the adult sense of rhythm imposed on them in this way.

Teachers use the lyre, or children's harp, in the classroom because of its gentle purity of tone. Influenced by its soft sound, the children's sense of hearing is heightened and becomes attuned to tone quality and pitch. When I taught a mixed-age class, I would sometimes allow the children to hold and play the lyre, showing them how to make the "wind" by stroking their fingers over the strings. The children found this a magical experience, and I learned much about the children as I watched their approach to the instrument. Some were timid, almost afraid to make a sound, some tried to produce tones as loudly as possible, others seemed to have an innate sense for the gesture which would produce a harmonious "wind" sound.

Of course children's experiences in the world of music are not limited to their hours at school, and it would not be realistic to expect that they would never hear any other kind of music. In our family, for example, my husband is a professional musician and I also played an instrument, so our children grew up surrounded with classical music. One day, many years ago, I decided to take my cello to school and play for the children in my class, thinking this would be a good experience for them. As it turned out, this was something I never repeated. The cello seemed so out of place in the classroom, so large and so loud; and what was Mrs. Foster doing play-ing that thing?! It was completely out of context.

In the Waldorf primary years the children are introduced to other instruments, and their experiences are broadened. In the early childhood years, we can lay the foundation for these experiences through allowing the children plenty of opportunity to hear and use the singing voice and to explore the world of sound freely through play. We can also take care that as parents we think carefully about the sounds and styles of music to which we expose our children. Just as we protect our children from stories which are too powerful for their stage of development, we should be conscious of protecting them from music which may be fine for adults but which is overstimulating or overpowering for the more delicate senses of the young child. If we can preserve, protect, and nourish the sense of hearing from the earliest years of a child's life, we will do much to ensure that he or she will have the capacity to live fully in the world of sound and music throughout the rest of life.

Work and Play at School

The Rhythm of the Morning

Question

When I first heard about Waldorf education, I had the impression that it was a gentle, non-coercive, play-oriented approach to school for young children. I was surprised, when I visited a class, that the morning seemed so highly structured. It seemed that there were a lot of expectations for the children. My child is happy there, but I still wonder about this seeming contradiction.

Answer

Betty Staley, an experienced Waldorf educator, has written a book about adolescence entitled *Between Form and Freedom*. It has occurred to me that the title has a certain relevance for every stage of life, though the meaning of "freedom" may change somewhat.

Experience shows us that young children are able to play most creatively and freely when they are provided with a form—or one could also say, a rhythm—which provides a sense of security. The morning at Acorn Hill has a definite rhythm, based on the in and out of the human breath. This morning rhythm alternates between the expansion or out-breath of free play, indoors and out, and the contraction or in-breath of group times, such as circle time and story time. Once the children have internalized this rhythm, they feel comfortable in it; knowing what to expect allows them to participate freely and wholeheartedly in the moment, assured that their involvement will not be interrupted by sudden, unexpected demands. When the children are "held" by a familiar form, they can be free within that form. Coercion is rarely an issue, though firmness can certainly be necessary in some cases.

Applying the principle of "freedom within form" to other stages of life, we could consider the case of the baby who has learned to crawl. It is well known how important it is for babies to be able to move freely and to explore their environment. How free is the baby, however, if the mother constantly has to run after it to prevent its falling down the stairs, or pulling a lamp over, and so forth? Won't the baby actually have more freedom if there is a protected area (for example, a gated room, or even, for short periods of time, a playpen) in which the baby can move freely yet safely, so there is not the need for constant interruption?

As adults, most of us have probably experienced the frustration of a much-anticipated free day, when we end up feeling the time has been wasted and we have not even enjoyed the freedom. The complete lack of form can be disorienting; even a minimal amount of structure will result in a more pleasant day. (Of course, adults vary widely in their "comfort zone" between form and freedom.)

Returning to the question of the classroom, I remember one observer's comment that the children seemed to move as if choreographed by an unseen director. The rhythm of the morning appeared to this observer to flow along gently and without coercion, leaving the children free to be children. This is our hope for the experience we offer the children.

Saying "You may..."

Question

The teachers at Acorn Hill seem to try very hard to speak clearly and properly, thereby increasing children's opportunity to understand what is being said and imitate correctly-spoken words. However, there appears to be a practice of saying "you may" to children when the intent is to give them a directive, for example, "You may put the stones away now." Please explain why this is the case.

Answer

The phrase "you may" originated with one of our mentors, who felt that with its use we actually encourage the children to do what they are able to do. In other words, we are saying, in effect, "You are five years old, and are strong and know where these stones belong, so now you may use your capacities to do what is needed." This thinking is based on the assumption that children generally feel a satisfaction in doing what they are able to do, and they should be encouraged to do things for the sake of the doing rather than to please us.

For this reason also we should take care not to praise children too much, but rather allow them to experience satisfaction in a deed or process. Giving orders, and praising, can have the effect of separating children from their wholehearted, unselfconscious activity. Young children naturally assume they are doing something well, to the best of their ability; it is not until the stage of first puberty, in the final year before first grade, that a healthy child has any doubt of this. Praise can raise the question prematurely.

All this said, however, the phrase "you may" can be overused and can become classroom jargon. The attitude behind the words is certainly more important than the words themselves. With the younger children, I often like to say, "Let's put the stones in the basket," because these little ones most often do actually need help in carrying out directions. It is realistic, and supportive of their learning, for them to feel that the adult is accompanying them rather than giving an order. In time, the children will become more independent and capable of carrying through with a task—then, "you may" will have real meaning.

Ironing in the Classroom: Danger?

Question

I understand the intent to model a domestic environment by including certain household tools. But why, considering the danger of burns and recognizing that this is an electric (not a manual) tool, do you choose to operate and have parents operate an iron in the classroom, and so close to where children are playing?

Answer

In my experience in kindergarten, nursery, and parent/child classes, I have found that when an adult is ironing, a mood of cozy contentment can permeate the nearby play. Some children are drawn to watch or to imitate, using a wooden iron or merely a piece of wood, while others play peacefully and purposefully on other themes. While it is true that our irons are heated by electricity, the essence of the activity remains: The one who irons is rhythmically moving the iron back and forth, smoothing/pressing the fabric.

By way of contrast, one can see that a vacuum cleaner, though it requires the same gesture as a carpet sweeper, is noisy; and a dishwasher not only creates noise, but substitutes the push of a button for the human activities of washing and rinsing, the experience of soapy water, and so forth. In ironing, it is probably the rhythmical, soothing quality of the activity which makes it such a harmonious and harmonizing activity in the classroom. Also, in my case, ironing is something I have always enjoyed, and we have observed that our attitude toward our activity has an effect on the children around us.

To be sure, the teacher or parent who is ironing must be alert to the issue of safety and must not leave the iron unattended on the ironing board. In our classroom there is a high shelf close by; if I need to go to another part of the room, I can quickly unplug the iron and place it safely out of reach. Furthermore, it is possible that on a particular day the children might be agitated and need more attention than usual, and a teacher might decide that it would be best not to use the iron. I can recall days when I spent much of the play time at the ironing board, while on other days it was necessary to stop after a shorter time in order to attend to the children in a different way.

The issue of danger is an interesting one. Looking around our classrooms and playground one sees a number of potential dangers: rocks can be (and have been) dropped on toes; heavy stumps can (and sometimes do) pinch fingers; playstands can (and do) fall over on a child; shovels can, if carelessly or wrongly wielded, hit or even cut another child; fingers can be caught in a cupboard door; and so on. We try to be alert and prevent accidents; nevertheless, accidents do happen. My view of this is that living in fear of danger is not an attitude to life which I want to model for the children. Life is full of risks, but a positive attitude of respect for this reality, along with a determination to do our best at prevention, seems to me the best way to approach this fact. Creating a totally danger-free environment is probably impossible, even if it were desirable. In actuality, children learn from accidents, and pain (within reason, of course) teaches them about the qualities of the surrounding world, about limits, respect, responsibility, and care for themselves and others. The adults' response to the inevitable accidents can teach the children that help is available, that distress can be met with calm and loving care, and that things can be put to rights again. These are important lessons for children to learn, and can help them to face life's challenges with confidence. In the end, the issue of safety is a matter of common sense, it seems to me, and a matter of making conscious choices about the kind of environment we seek to create for our children, at home and at school.

Boys and Waldorf Education

Question

I suspect that Waldorf education doesn't work well for active boys, and Waldorf schools really don't want boys unless they are passive. Is this true?

Answer

This concern, which has been voiced by more than one person, raises a variety of questions. Confining our considerations to the nursery and kindergarten level, what might contribute to such a view of Waldorf education? Putting myself into a parent's place, I can imagine several things.

Our classrooms are painted in shades of pink, from rosy to apricot— a stereotypical girls' color. While the classroom play equipment includes dolls and play dishes, there are no cars, trucks, airplanes, or rocket ships. We strongly discourage (and try to prevent) gun play and aggressive "gang" activity. We expect the children to stay seated at the snack table, to take part in circle time, and to sit quietly and attentively at story time. Perhaps these things give an impression that our environment is unsuitable for active boys.

Much could be said about the nursery/kindergarten environment and how it can nourish all children, and the question of cars and trucks was addressed earlier. For now, however, I would like to make some comments about the issue of activity level, because in my opinion, the needs of active children (boys and girls) can best be understood in the context of two larger questions: 1) what is the basis for our structuring of the nursery/kindergarten morning? and 2) what, in a general sense, is our goal for the children who come to our school? I will try to address these questions, in the hope of shedding some light on the concern about boys and Waldorf education.

1) We often compare our morning class schedule to the rhythm of breathing. In breathing, we experience on the most basic, life-sustaining level the polarity of contraction (breathing in) and expansion (breathing out). We can all experience the discomfort and anxiety if we are forced to

hold our breath too long. I remember all too well the difficulty I had as a child in trying to swim underwater across the pool. On the other hand, if we breathe out too long, such as in blowing up a balloon or laughing hysterically, we can become quite giddy and even lose consciousness. If our breathing is shallow, such as in panting rapidly, we feel stifled. We feel best when our breathing is deep and steady, with a rhythmical alternation of expansion and contraction.

Translating these experiences to the rhythm of the morning, we allow the children to experience an alternation of active and more quiet times—of times when they choose their own activities and move freely about the room or play outdoors, and times when the group comes together in more quiet, focused activity. During creative indoor play the children may build a farm with the wood pieces, stones, and knitted animals; or move the play stands and erect a house or space ship; or move the heavy stumps onto the rug to use as stepping or jumping equipment; or they may create a restaurant in the play house; or take the "babies" for a picnic. This is a time of out-breathing—of free and active play. Story time, on the other hand, is an in-breathing, when the children sit quietly and watch or listen as the teacher tells a fairy tale or nature story. Experience shows us that children thrive best when they are not expected to spend too long at either extreme of in- or out-breathing. Of course, given the active nature of the young child, the in-breathing times need to be shorter than the out-breathing; in the course of the morning a sense of balance is achieved.

Depending on the nature of a particular child, one or the other pole of expansion or contraction may prove to be more challenging. A quiet, introverted child may at first feel overwhelmed by the activity level of creative play, indoors or outdoors, and may need to stay close to the teacher for a while. A very active or restless child, whether a boy or a girl, will find more difficulty in settling down into a time of in-breathing, and, again, may need extra support from the teacher.

2) The foregoing comments about the nature of individual children lead to the second question, regarding our goal for the children in the nursery and kindergarten. In a very general sense, we might say that the foremost activity for the young child in school is socialization—that is to say, learning to become a social being as a preparation for life among other human beings. It is our responsibility as parents and teachers to guide the children in our care into the experience of harmonious living. One important quality of harmonious living is a healthy rhythm of expansion and contraction. While each of us, as an adult, must find the particular rhythm that suits us, we all do need to find a balance between these two poles.

If we were to allow, or compel, these young children to stay too long at either extreme, they would become quite distressed. Our observations over the years bear this out and can, I am sure, be confirmed by most parents. Children who are expected to sit still for too long will eventually "explode;" on the other hand, if they run about without focus or guidance for too long, they become over-excited and, finally, exhausted. The over-tired child who has a temper tantrum is an example of this phenomenon.

Therefore, while it is not always easy for a young child to accept the transition from one pole to the other, and while an active child may resist settling into a time of in-breathing, the need to do this is part of the process of socialization, of learning. In fact, it is one of the earliest, most important lessons we can offer to our children. We would do them a disservice not to guide them into a healthy rhythm. Throughout our lives we must be able to adapt to the needs of a situation, and these early experiences lay the groundwork for the capacity to do so.

Playing Cats and Dogs

Question

While observing a class, I saw children who wanted to be cats and dogs, and the teacher told them they needed to have a master, who would teach them to "sit," etc. Some children were glad to be "masters," but the "cats and dogs" seemed to be having less fun. What is the thinking behind this approach?

Answer

In my experience, cat and dog play in the classroom is rarely constructive or imaginative. It tends to involve a lot of crawling or scrambling around on the floor, with high-pitched, squealing noise which permeates the whole room. It does not seem that the children are really experiencing "cat-ness"—for example the stealthy prowl, the delicate paws, the satisfied purring, the quick pounce—but rather they seem to have descended to a wilder, primal state of chaos! There is nothing wrong with healthy noise and active movement, if it is in service of constructive play and leads to a sense of satisfaction for the children. Cat and dog play, however, often seems to become compulsive and to degenerate into noise and activity without purpose.

This situation can be handled in various ways, depending on the particular group of children and the teacher's perception of their needs. This may differ quite a bit from one situation or one group to another. I have had groups in which a child or two seemed to have a need to be a cat during play time, and this cat was easily and naturally incorporated into the other children's play. In such cases, in which it was a genuine need for that child—for whatever reason—this was not "catching" and did not result in the chaotic situation described above. In other groups, I have had to absolutely forbid cat play because it always destroyed the mood of constructive activity in the room.

In some situations, such as the one you observed, the teacher may redirect the play so that some children become masters of the cats or dogs, and this can often be successful in transforming the activity into role playing or dramatic play, since it creates a context for something to "happen." The thinking behind this approach can perhaps be explained as follows.

In addition to the fundamental task in the first six or seven years of life—that of physical growth and development—socialization is a primary aspect of the infant's and child's life and experience. Socialization can be characterized as the process of becoming human, of learning, very gradually, how to recognize the needs of other human beings or of a situation, and to adapt one's behavior appropriately to meet these needs and expectations. It could also be described as the process of gaining mastery over impulses, learning, for example, to wait to eat until the verse has been said, or not to grab a toy from another child. In this context, one could picture the cats as representing the impulsive or instinctive nature of the child, and the master as the growing capacity to direct the impulses. This mastery is something which needs to be supported and encouraged in many ways, as appropriate to the age of the particular children.

In the preschool years, the most important support to mastery is given through rhythm, repetition, and the child's capacity to imitate. In the grade school years, the process continues through the child's acceptance of the teacher as the loved authority. It has been observed that older kindergarten children may wish to play cat or dog and to have a master, thus indicating their approach toward readiness for the grade school experience.

I should perhaps mention, finally, that it sometimes happens that a child or group of children becomes "stuck" in one form of play, and the observant teacher will make note of this and try to help the children find a new direction. I remember one little girl who, after the birth of a baby sister, played baby every day for weeks. At first, I thought this was probably a healthy way for her to work through this new experience, and her playmates were happy to oblige. I assumed that she would soon be satisfied and move on to other kinds of play. However, the baby play kept on, and

I noticed she did not seem very happy. Finally I made a decision, and one morning, with some trepidation—fearing a fit of sulking or distress—I let her know that the baby wouldn't be coming to school any more, and that she could be a big sister now. She actually looked quite relieved, and from that moment on was her former happy, creative, social five-year-old self. She had somehow become stuck in playing out a regression, and was grateful for the help in extricating herself so that she could proceed in her development.

This can also happen with cat and dog play; it can seem that the children are caught in a regressive form of behavior, when actually they would find other forms of play much more satisfying. Play in which they are modeling themselves on adult roles is really the most healthy for their development, and they generally sense this and appreciate guidance and encouragement from time to time. Playing mother and father, fireman, auto mechanic, teacher, baker, fisherman, office worker (using wood slices for computers or fax machines!). . . this is the way the children "play themselves into" the world of being human.

Music in the Mood of the Fifth

Question

Can you explain music in the mood of the fifth, how it affects the young child, why it is important, and how the non-musically-knowledgeable can become aware of it and use it in their own singing?

Answer

Mood of the fifth music is a fairly recent development in the field of music, and I first began learning about it in the early 1980's. It is based on Rudolf Steiner's insights into the nature and development of the young child in the context of music history as it reflects the development of human consciousness. Without going into unnecessary technical detail, it can be said that this music swings around the note A above middle C, creating a sense of pure openness. This could be compared to the movement of a see-saw, with the two riders moving up and down on each side of a fulcrum (in this case, the note A). Several notes may be used, but the general shape of the melody will create a sense of balance around the A. An example is given below. This music may at first seem strange to adults, since we are accustomed to music with a stronger sense of direction—music which is in a particular key, such as "Twinkle, Twinkle, Little Star" and most of the other songs we all grew up with, as well as most of the traditional or popular music we hear around us. It takes time for us to become comfortable with music in the mood of the fifth.

This music is appropriate and healing for the young child, who still lives in a condition of pure openness and receptivity to all the surroundings—one might say in wholehearted participation or empathy. Music in the mood of the fifth, with its balanced simplicity, leaves the child free to "sing itself into life," rather than imposing a more compelling tone progression. The rhythm of this music tends to be freely flowing, rather than strongly rhythmic or march-like, thus also allowing the child a certain inner freedom. In today's world, with its many stimulating sights and sounds bombarding the child's delicate senses from every side, this music can be experienced as soothing and, at the same time, enlivening.

In my classroom I have not limited the music to mood of the fifth. I feel there is a place for other songs, as long as they are of good quality. Simple folk melodies are particularly suitable. A healing mood can be achieved with this music too, especially if the adult takes care to sing with a light, clear tone that can be easily imitated by the child. Still, I have made it a practice that the songs we sing every day—for example, at the beginning of circle time, before the story, and at the end of the morning— are in the mood of the fifth. Thus this music provides the basic framework around which other songs may be woven.

For the "non-musically-knowledgeable," it is certainly not necessary to know the technical aspects of this kind of music. It can be learned and sung in the same way as any other songs. The most important thing is that the child sense our enjoyment of singing, whether our voice is particularly lovely or not. Because mood of the fifth music is fairly new, there is not a lot available. One source is the two volumes of the "Acorn Hill Anthology:" *Let Us Form a Ring*, and *Dancing As We Sing*. Another, more recently published, is *I Love to be Me* by Channa Seidenberg. Still another source is the Wynstones early childhood collection of songs, poems, and stories, which includes many songs in the mood of the fifth.

Below is an example of a song in the mood of the fifth, which illustrates the sense of balancing around the note A.

Can Energetic Boys Enjoy Handwork?

Question

How does Waldorf education regard "boy energy" in relation to the emphasis on crafts and fine motor skills, given that boys typically have less interest than girls in these?

Answer

When the first Waldorf School opened in Germany in 1919, it was considered quite radical that boys and girls were to share classes as well as all aspects of the curriculum. It is still the case that the Waldorf curriculum is the same for both sexes from nursery through high school. In a Waldorf grade school and high school, boys and girls learn to knit and sew, do woodwork and bookbinding, sculpt in clay and stone, garden, play a musical instrument, participate in eurythmy and spatial dynamics, and even, in some schools, learn blacksmithing, as well as taking up the usual academic subjects. In a nursery and kindergarten, both boys and girls have the opportunity to play, sing, bake, paint and draw, learn to fingerknit and sew, work with wood, use scissors and glue, hear and tell stories, garden, and so on.

Contemporary brain research confirms what has long been known to Waldorf educators, thanks to Rudolf Steiner's insights: the child's physical organism is actually shaped by the activities and movements engaged in by the young child. The brain and neurological system are elaborated and equipped for later intellectual learning, and the integration of the sensory organism lays the basis for the ability to function as a balanced individual. It is therefore essential that every child have ample opportunities for both large- and small-muscle activity, and this is what we provide in Waldorf education. Clearly, the activity must be age-appropriate, and we take care that all activities in the nursery and kindergarten are in proportion to the whole, within a rhythm of in-breathing (more focused activity) and out-breathing (more active, free-flowing times).

What is "boy energy?" At a recent parent evening, the topic of gun play arose, and a number of parents commented on their observation that this seems to be almost exclusively a boy activity. While we can surely all agree that boys and girls are of equal value as individuals, those of us who spend time with young children are unlikely to assert that they are the same in terms of their play. Given the fact that every child is unique, with his or her particular temperament, constitution, preferences, personality—however one wishes to characterize such qualities—it is still possible to notice gender differences. Perhaps we could generalize by saying that boys tend to be more expansive and energetic in their play than girls, on the whole—again, always leaving room for individual differences. Some people call this "boy energy," and it is true that some boys will prefer active, large-muscle play to fine-motor activities such as crafts and handwork. We know, also, that at this age boys are generally about six months "behind" girls developmentally. Thus fine motor activities may be more difficult for them. It is important for both boys and girls to be able to engage in, and enjoy, both kinds of activities, and we try to work toward this goal without forcing children. The younger the child, the more free we leave him or her to play in his or her own "style." As the child approaches first grade age, however, we feel it is important to make sure that the child has a chance to develop the capacities that will be called on in the grades and later. We thus encourage the child's participation in activities which are developmentally appropriate (for example, jumping rope outdoors, and sewing or painting indoors) and which will help in the child's growth, forming the basis for grade school experiences.

I have wonderful memories, from my years as a teacher of mixed-age kindergarten, of hearty, vigorous boys who were able to focus that energy and enthusiasm for a shorter or longer period of time on a craft or handwork activity. They cut out stars in their lanterns, dressed wooden "pirates" to sail on the wooden ships they had made, took great pleasure in their developing control of paint colors, embroidered treasure bags—and were just as wholehearted in the construction of space ships, racing vehicles, and, yes, "traps for the bad guys." In a Waldorf preschool, our aim is not to suppress boy energy, but to meet it with warmth and energy of our own, helping the boys to channel their energy into constructive activity of many kinds.

Gun Play at School

Question

What is the attitude toward gun play in the classrooms at Acorn Hill? As a parent of a boy, I am troubled by this issue. While I don't encourage or even approve of gun play, it seems to come so naturally to my son. I don't want him to be labeled, by teachers or other parents, as a "bad boy."

Answer

I too have noticed that many boys seem to turn easily to gun play, even if toy guns are not available. They will use anything that comes to hand: sticks, logs, wooden spoons, corncobs, or even a finger. Sometimes these gun substitutes are used in an aggressive manner, while at other times they seem to serve more as a security item.

I have also noticed what an emotional issue this can be for adults. Our horror at the violence in the world at large and in our own society is projected into this issue of children's play, making it hard for us to confront the question with the interest and objectivity it deserves. I also sense a great deal of fear—fear that our child will turn out to be violent and aggressive, fear that our child will be frightened or victimized by other children, fear that we won't know how to handle the situation.

As far as the classroom goes, I believe all of our teachers discourage gun play; for example, they may say, "We don't have guns at school." I will speak here of my own experiences and approach. Other teachers may, of course, have different approaches.

When I taught a mixed-age class, I did not allow gun play, and children were not allowed to point anything at another child. With many groups of children, this did not seem to be a problem. In some groups, however, the children became adept at trying to deceive me in this regard. For example, they would build a spaceship out of play stands, with logs projecting on every side. They claimed these were telescopes, yet it was obvious that they were actually guns. Or, they would carry wood pieces around in gun-like fashion, but when confronted, insist that they were flashlights. Eventually I decided that it was worse, in a moral sense, for these children to be learning deceit than it would be for them to play with these imaginary guns—as long as they did not point them at others. So I began to tolerate such play; but if these guns were aimed at people, I immediately took them away. I also did not allow play that was totally centered on guns, or roving "gangs," etc. This of course was always a judgment call, but the mood or intent of the play was generally pretty clear. To the older children, I would sometimes say, "We don't point guns at people; guns can hurt people, and I don't like that" (or words to that effect). It seemed to me important that the older children know that I was taking a stand about guns, since they were of an age to begin to consider the world of morality in a conscious way.

In the nursery class, gun play also occurs, but not in the more elaborate form of the older children (the building of spaceships, battleships, etc.). With these younger children, it is usually a matter of carrying wood pieces around, being "hunters," or verbalizing a theme of "shooting the bad guys." Impulsive as these young ones are, I have found it does little good to make general rules; rather, I need to deal with each particular situation as it arises. As with the older children, I do not allow them to point objects at other children, and if they do, I remove the object (stick, log, or whatever). In some groups of children, where there is an especially strong urge toward this behavior, I have sometimes simply removed the crate of logs from the classroom.

Often, in the nursery class, the mention of shooting, or actually playing guns, is fairly fleeting—a characteristic of the generally fluid, changeable play at this age. In such cases, I may simply ignore it, knowing that it will soon pass by. The nature of the particular child or children involved must also be taken into account. For example, I remember a small boy who, during outdoor play time, was never seen without a stick ("gun") clutched in his hand. He never did anything with the gun, and knowing this child, we realized he would have been completely devastated if we had demanded that he relinquish this weapon. For him, this was a security item, his only means of protection in the (to him) overwhelming largeness and boisterousness of the play area. In his following years at Acorn Hill, the gun disappeared and he was able to take part in outdoor play with confidence and enjoyment.

It can be painful for parents when a child comes home talking about guns or shooting, perhaps for the first time. As parents, we can feel sad or even angry that our child has been exposed to such play. Or, if it is our child who is the gun-player, we can feel ashamed of what other parents will think of us. These feelings are very understandable, and I have no easy answers to any of this. All I can offer are the following thoughts.

1. As with any parenting and teaching issue that confronts us, our first task is to think through the issue and try to reach a place of calm understanding and objectivity in ourselves. If we react out of our own emotion or discomfort or insecurity, the child will absorb our feelings and become confused, resistant, or upset; feelings of guilt may also result.

2. Remember that for children, play fulfills the role that thinking plays for adults. That is, it is the way children explore the world, learn about the world, and work through their experiences. Children "play out" their experiences of their environment and also their inner experiences. This is a fascinating topic in itself, but all parents can observe this in their children. This play is important, even essential, in order for children to make sense of their world and to move on to new experiences, new learning. Playing with guns, or play which involves death, may be the result of involvement in a particular life situation, of hearing adult conversation, or of imitating other children. Or, as already mentioned, it may seem to come naturally to a child. (Why this seems to be so for so many boys is another fascinating topic.) Nevertheless, it is our responsibility as adults to be aware of, and, if necessary, to guide our children's play. If it seems to become compulsive or obsessive, whatever the theme or activity, we must try to find a way to redirect or even stop the play. I have seen situations in the classroom when the children actually seemed relieved when this was

done; it was almost as if they had become locked into a kind of play and did not know how to transform it and move ahead.

3. Try to keep this issue in perspective. Think back to your own childhood: did you ever play cowboys and Indians, cops and robbers, war? I certainly did—even though I was brought up in a pacifist family. And you and I have not ended up thinking that violence and aggression are the appropriate approach to problem-solving. I suspect that our children, too, will become adults with healthy social impulses, if we can be good models for them.

4. Protect your children from exposure to TV news programs, which all too often feature reports of crime and violence. These young children are not able to make sense of such images. When they are older, it will be possible to begin to discuss these things with them, but this is not the time. Their understanding is not yet ripe. If your child does come in contact with violence—such as a crime in your neighborhood—try to handle this calmly. We cannot shield our children completely from such things, perhaps; but we can emphasize for them the role of those who step in to be of help in these situations, and assure them that we are there to take care of them. 🌺

Field Trips?

Question

Why don't you ever take the children on field trips?

Answer

In a sense, one could say we do go on field trips, since the five-day classes have "walk day" each week when they go to the park for outdoor play time. This gives them an opportunity to walk, to explore another natural environment, and to expand their horizons beyond the school grounds. This is an enjoyable part of their school experience. In the sense of taking the children by car or bus to museums, parks, playgrounds, or fairs, however, we do not take field trips. In the past, some classes did go to a farm each Halloween to pick pumpkins, and a few times we even returned in the spring to see the farm and take a hay ride—until the farmer, one year, showed the children the seed corn, which was ghastly pink because of the chemicals with which it had been treated, and pointed out the brown, dead weeds in the fields, which had been sprayed with herbicides and pesticides. These trips were in the days before car seats were obligatory and before serious concern about insurance. Logistics of planning were complicated enough then. Nowadays, it would be even more complicated. In any case, we realized that for young children, such trips are much more relaxed and pleasurable if they are not with a large group, but are taken with their own family, so that they can be more free to experience things at their own pace.

In addition, many children already spend too much time being taken here and there in the car. At this age, we feel, trips to the museum, the zoo, or the amusement park are far less important than the opportunity for the children to have time to become acquainted with what is in their home environment. As one experienced Waldorf educator said, the "zoo in your own backyard" is much more meaningful to a small child than looking at elephants and tigers in cages. Still less relevant to their experience are museums. I remember the five-year-old child of a friend, who said, upon being told they were going to a natural history museum: "But I want to see the animals that move!" This same city child had a wonderful time at a playground, collecting a jar full of tent caterpillars.

Watching ants, digging for earthworms, planting a small garden, sweeping the sidewalk, raking leaves. . . these experiences, close to home, help a small child to feel at home in the world and to form a bond with the world of nature. Later there will be plenty of time to move out into the wider world. Of course, children in an urban environment, who may not have even a small yard, will need to be taken regularly to a park, if at all possible. Even so, however, it will be good if they can return over and over again to the same park, so that they can really become familiar and at home with it in all weather and in all seasons. Allowing a child to become deeply connected with a place will support the child's sense of security and enhance the capacity for attentiveness and wonder.

Fairy Tales for Young Children

Question

I am aware that you tell some of the Grimm's fairy tales at Acorn Hill, and I'm concerned with the incidence of violence in the stories. I'm also concerned that in some of the stories "good" seems to be equated with "beautiful" and "bad" with "ugly." These are not values I want my child to be absorbing. Why do you tell these stories?

Answer

We tell some of these fairy tales because we believe they provide an important basis for human life. However, it is important to choose carefully what fairy tales are told, according to the age of the child. The younger the child, the more simple the story should be, and the more benign the challenges or evil to be overcome. Most children are not ready for any fairy tales until around age four, when the capacity for fantasy has become established.

Children who are ready for fairy tales instinctively know that these stories are not literally true on the physical plane, but are true pictures of inner events and circumstances, of inner challenges and forces which must be faced and overcome. Thus, they sense that beauty and ugliness refer to inner qualities, not external appearance. If the story is age-appropriate and told in a matter-of-fact, nondramatized way, the child will be able to hear and digest it without the "baggage" of adult feelings or intellectual interpretation. It is important for the storyteller to be familiar with the story, and to enjoy it.

If you don't like a particular fairy tale or it makes you uncomfortable, it will not be good for your child. By living with the story for a while and searching for its deeper meaning, rather than looking at it in a literal way, you may come to feel differently about it.

You should also be aware of the issue of authenticity. Some children's versions of the classic tales have been revised; you should avoid such versions, since the whole point of the story is often lost or altered. The quality of illustrations too should be considered and cartoon-like depictions avoided. Even beautiful, artistic drawings may be better saved for older children, since they may emphasize the strong emotions of the tales and be overpowering for young children. The most authentic version of the Grimm's tales can be found in the Pantheon edition edited by Padraic Colum. The literary fairy tales, written by a known author rather than handed down through the oral tradition, include those by Hans Christian Andersen and Oscar Wilde; these are suitable for older children or even adults, but not for young children.

In regard to the issue of violence and evil, it is a reality that children, and all of us, do encounter challenges and bad or frightening experiences in life. The fairy tales, in which such experiences are redeemed in various ways according to the particular story, help to give children the trust that challenges can be overcome and that we are not powerless.

To this could be added the following thoughts. As parents we must, from the moment a child is born, go through a life-long process of "letting go." It is an enormous challenge to fi nd the balance between protection and allowing the child to meet and face the obstacles which alone make possible growth and development. (A simple analogy: our muscles grow strong only through resistance.) Our aim should not be to shield our children from challenges or even danger; otherwise we, and they, would live in a state of paralysis. Rather, we should do the best we can in our life circumstances to ensure that the challenges and danger are appropriate and not overwhelming. We need to realize, however, that we do not have total control over life. Things happen: accidents, death, emotional upsets. These things are part of life, and it is important, when they happen, that children have the experience that we deal with them as best we can. The fairy tales are a wonderful source of strength in this regard.

Furthermore, most of us are familiar with the concept that if we can name something that threatens or frightens us, it loses its power over us. It occurs to me that fairy tales provide this quality of "naming." Each story offers an image of a particular danger or obstacle to be overcome—i.e. it gives the danger a name. The story allows us to see, to become famil-iar with, to name, an inner or outer challenge and thus to confront it. This is the way we grow and fi nd our way through life. By telling our children these age-old, wise tales, we offer them a fount of wisdom and support for life. ❧

The Challenge of Circle Time

Question

Recently I observed a five-day class and noticed at circle time that the older boys did not seem engaged and, in fact, were quite disruptive. Do you think the circles are oriented more to girls, so the boys just don't enjoy them?

Answer

Not having seen the particular situation, I can't really give a specific answer. I can, however, address the question in a more general way by mentioning some factors that might have been involved in what you saw.

First we might look at the children's response to circle itself. I still remember a eurythmy teacher from Europe, years ago, who exclaimed indignantly, "Kindergarten teachers always make their circles too 'airy-fairy'!" This made a strong impression on me, and I think teachers now are more aware of the need to offer a balance of experiences at circle time. We speak of using "polarities"—quiet/boisterous, fast/slow, serious/humorous. For example, in a spring circle we may be birds and butterflies for a while, but then we skip in the rain and jump in the puddles. Or, in a winter circle we may take big, energetic strides through the deep snow, but then we stop and listen for the wind. Without these polarities, the children easily feel out of balance or over-extended, and can lose their focus and become disruptive. Of course the balance can also happen over time, so that one particular circle may go more in the direction of quiet and another may be in general more lively.

A particular child may feel more comfortable at one pole of activity than the other. For example, a child who feels ill at ease with fast, energetic movement may try to leave the circle at such times; one who finds it hard to reach a quiet, peaceful mood may rebel when this is called for. Part of the kindergarten experience is learning gradually to "breathe" between moods and levels of activity. This is a process, and it applies to both girls and boys. It has often been observed that boys are more likely than girls to exhibit a need for energetic activity, and teachers should be aware of this in planning circle time. However, both poles of experience are needed by both genders.

We could also look at the developmental level of the children, since you mentioned older boys. Sometime between the ages of about 5 1/2 and 6 1/2, children usually go through a stage we call first puberty, because it is a bit like a foretaste of early adolescence. Before this stage, children are naturally imitative on an instinctive level, and they are (or should generally be) able to play in a fantasy-filled way, transforming the materials available into whatever is needed: a tree stump may be a train car, a stepping stone, a table in a restaurant, or an ironing board. In first puberty, the child begins to grow out of this fantasy stage; inwardly there is a sense of confusion, of being neither a little child nor a big child. This sense of discomfort, rather like the adolescent who is neither child nor adult and cannot quite find his place, shows itself in various ways—complaints of boredom, the inability to play happily and imaginatively, out-of-bounds behavior and rebellion, or excessive silliness or sulkiness. This stage, necessary in achieving first-grade readiness, is to be welcomed, even though it may make life at home or school more difficult for a time. It may last for only a week or two, or may go on for months, depending on the child. A child in this stage often has great difficulty participating in circle because he can no longer imitate freely and unselfconsciously. When this stage passes, the child generally regains harmony.

There are, of course, other factors which might influence a child's behavior at circle time, and teachers always do their best to try to discern and meet the needs of a particular group of children or of individual children. ❧

Puppetry and "Told" Stories

Question

When my daughter was in the two- and three-day classes, the teacher gave puppet plays every day. Now, in the five-day class, she sees fewer puppet plays, and she misses them. She plays with her own puppets at home constantly, and sometimes says she wishes she were back in the three-day class. Are there any guidelines about how often a teacher should present puppet plays during the year?

Answer

In the nursery classes at Acorn Hill we do present a puppet or marionette play at story time most, though not all, of the time. As you know, the children see the same story for a block of time, usually about three weeks, so that they can experience the story very deeply. These younger children are generally developmentally unready to follow a narrative without visual images or gestures because they are not yet able to form mental pictures at will. The simple forms and colors, the movement and gestures of the puppets or marionettes, the rhythm and mood of the teacher's voice—these allow the children to enter into the story with their whole being.

In a mixed-age class, the older children are becoming able to form mental images to accompany a narrative. It is, in fact, very important for them to develop and exercise this capacity as a part of their journey toward readiness for "academic" schooling, when mental imaging will be crucial for following teachers' instructions and absorbing the experiences offered at school. Thus, "told" stories are both important and satisfying for children. One could say that these stories leave the children free to create their own pictures. We may have a sense of the living, vivid quality of such inner pictures if we can recall seeing a movie of a book we have read, finding ourselves exclaiming, "But that's not how she looked!" The youngest children listening to a "told" story in a mixed-age group, even if not quite able yet to follow a narrative on their own, are carried along by the mood of the group and by the rhythm of the storyteller's voice, as well as the repetition over a period of time. One can imagine images, not too clearly formed, drifting across their inner vision like rosy clouds. . . and imagine the children's delight if they should be able to hear the same story the next year, somehow familiar, yet different, more clearly pictured, because of their newly awakening capacities.

As to how many puppet plays a particular teacher may offer, there is no rule. Each teacher tries to find a balance between plays and "told" stories that seems suitable to a particular group, to her own affinity for certain stories, and to the cycle of seasons. And it is a wonderful thing when children build up their own puppet plays at home or at school, sometimes re-telling a story they have seen and heard, sometimes creating their own. We certainly wish to encourage this kind of play, while at the same time we try to avoid making the children self-conscious by requesting performances. ❧

Children at
Home

Colors for a Child's Bedroom

Question

I'm considering painting my children's rooms and would like more information on the effects that various colors have on children. For instance, I love a nice light blue, but understand that's not necessarily appropriate for a five-year-old. Please help!

Answer

You are right that it's good to consider a child's needs rather than our own preference when deciding on the color for the child's room. There are a couple of ways you could approach the issue.

Some children have, from the beginning, a predilection for a particular color. In that case, it may be a good thing to paint the bedroom in that shade. This will give your child a sense of comfort which will be strengthening and nurturing in these early years.

It is best, however, not to ask your child if he or she has a favorite color. The above approach is useful only if color preference is obvious; you would not want to bring the issue to your child's awareness, in effect asking the child to make a decision which would be much too weighty. It is challenging enough for us as adults to choose a room color.

If there is not a clear color preference, you could consider your child's nature. While temperament generally does not become well established until around the age of seven (though in some cases it may be present earlier), you can certainly identify tendencies in one direction or another. Rudolf Steiner tells us that a color calls up its complement in the child, rather like the after-image effect we obtain by looking at a color and then looking at a white surface, on which we will see the same shape in the complementary color.

With this in mind, you could consider the following: If your child is of a lively, outgoing, active, or forceful nature, you might paint the room yellow or red. The yellow would call up its complement of violet; the complement of red is green. These colors would have a quieting, calming effect on your child. If, on the other hand, your child is quiet, placid, shy, or thoughtful, you might choose a shade of blue or green. The complement of blue is orange; the complement of green is red. These colors would have an enlivening effect. As I think about this idea, it makes sense to me that choosing a color which outwardly matches a child's nature would make the child feel at home, comfortable, thus beginning where the child is and then leading him or her inwardly into a balanced condition. In this way you are working with the child's nature instead of opposing it.

I think it is best not to paint a child's room in an intense color such as bright red, deep blue, etc. It seems to me this would be too strong for a child's developing senses and could give an uncomfortable effect of walls closing in. If a shade of red is what seems appropriate, for example, I would paint the walls in a warm but more delicate shade of rose or peach, which will create a gentle complement. It is also ideal if the color is not solid and opaque, but gives a sense of transparency. You may find an opportunity to learn how to create this effect, or to find someone who can. However, this is not always possible, and sensitivity to the color intensity can still give a beautiful result. If your child is drawn to strong colors, you could choose a rug or carpet and curtains in a deeper, brighter (but still not too harsh) shade of the same color as the wall.

Older and Younger Siblings

Question

For our older child, we were able to create an environment and provide activities which we felt were age-appropriate. It has been difficult to provide the same protection for our younger child. How can we allow the younger child the same time to "be young"—not to be drawn into and influenced by the needs of the older child?

Answer

As our sons were growing up, my husband and I found this to be one of the more difficult and frustrating issues we faced. It seemed that we were often caught between the proverbial "rock and a hard place." Our younger son would complain, "Why can't I have a watch? Ben has one!" Our older son would complain, "You didn't get me a watch until I was seven, but Daniel has one now, and he's only six!"

The issue of different-age siblings arises around the question of possessions and privileges, such as getting an allowance, being allowed to go on a sleep-over, staying up later in the evening, and so on. It also arises in terms of the younger child's exposure to the activities, interests, and attitudes of the older child. The issue takes on differing color and intensity depending on the age difference between siblings, too.

In our family, we eventually arrived at some ways to deal with these issues. First of all, we had to learn to be flexible rather than dogmatic, and to realize that ideals sometimes have to yield to circumstances. We also tried to look at the positive aspects of the situation. For example, it can be a very healthy thing for a younger child to have the sense that there are certain things he will be able to do, or have, when he is older. This is, in a subtle but essential way, different from the message, "You're too young." It both gives the older child a sense of responsibility and offers the younger child something to aspire to, to grow toward. A Waldorf educator said that one way of nurturing the sense of wonder is to allow a child to experience that there are certain things or places to which he doesn't have access

(Mother's special drawer, Father's cabinet, etc.). The same idea was conveyed when I taught a mixed-age class and allowed only the six-year-olds a turn to take a piece of birthday cake to the office staff.

It can also be helpful to acknowledge, without dwelling on, the frustrated feelings of the particular sibling: "Yes, I know it doesn't seem fair that Daniel has a watch already, but sometimes that's just how it is." (Perhaps you would find something more graceful to say, but the point is simply to show that the feeling is understandable, without going into all the why's and wherefore's, which belong only to the adult realm.) Or, to the younger sibling, you might say, "I know it's hard to wait, but you'll be able to have a watch when you're older." In either case, you are calmly and confidently affirming, "Yes, this is the situation."

Practical pointers to help in meeting the needs of children of different ages might center around opportunities to spend time alone with each child and to devote this time to an activity geared to that particular child's age and interests. This may need to involve some creative planning, arranging for one child to spend time with a friend, for example, while you are with the other child. For a younger child, the chance to take a walk with Mommy or Daddy without having to keep up with the older child can be a real gift. You might use a younger child's rest or nap time to do something special with the older child. If parent schedules can be worked out, it is ideal for each child to have a separate bedtime story and nighttime verse.

Dinnertime conversation and car rides can present severe challenges to the hope of protecting the innocence of a younger sibling. You may feel the topics of conversation introduced by big brother or sister are inappropriate for the younger child, and it may not always be reasonable to expect the older child to make such a judgment and be restrained. These situations require tact and presence of mind on your part. In a rare situation you might actually have to stop the older child and let him or her know you will talk more later. In many cases, though, it seems necessary to accept that the younger child's experience simply will be different from the older child's. Each family position has its advantages and disadvantages.

Just as important as honoring age differences is encouraging a sense of the wholeness of the family, in which each member plays a different, but equally valid, role. Each family member above infancy should have some responsibility for family life, according to the possibilities of his or her age. For the very young child, this may be something as small as helping Mommy or Daddy put the dolls to bed before supper, while the older child may be the one to set the table each evening, or take out the trash, and so forth. Developing a sense of mutual respect is also important. If a child feels his needs (as opposed to whims) are being recognized and met, he will be more able to accept the reality of others' needs.

Finally, with this issue, as with all parenting issues, the key is your own attitude to the situation. If you have thought about your goals for family life and how you plan to handle a particular issue, you will have the inner certainty you need to hold firm in the face of protests. You and your children will be able to take the unavoidable mistakes in stride. Your firmness, coupled with your genuine love for your children, will ultimately be of greatest importance to them. 🌿

Boredom

Question

When my daughter whines, "I'm bored," I really feel annoyed. We've made an effort to make sure she has plenty of toys and activities available. I also feel guilty; maybe I don't spend enough time with her. How much "playing with" or "entertaining" should be expected of a parent?

Answer

This question can be approached from two (at least!) different directions. First, we can look at the age of the child. Children between the ages of about 5 1/2 and 6 1/2 go through a stage we call first puberty. This may last from a few weeks to a few months, and, as the name implies, it is a foretaste of real adolescence and can be quite trying to both the child and the parents—and teachers, as well! If your daughter is in this age range, this is what she may be experiencing; compare notes with her teacher to help you find out. At this time, a child is making the transition from early childhood to school-age childhood, and, as at every life transition, there is a sense of unease, a loss of certainty. She realizes, unconsciously of course, that she is leaving the world of early childhood, but she has not yet reached the new stage. This leaves her feeling unsettled and dissatisfied with herself and with life in general. She loses her earlier capacity for fantasy play, and literally does not know what to do with herself. She may become defiant, or very silly, or unusually sulky and insecure; for some reason, many children express this by saying they are "bored."

During this stage, it is useless to try to suggest play themes or to get her interested in activities she formerly enjoyed. She is simply unable to play right now. Instead, this is the time to get her involved in real work. At school, for example, we might give her the task of taking all the toys off the shelf, washing and drying the shelf, and replacing the toys. Or we might ask her to help us saw wood to help build a bird feeder. At home she might be asked to help with dinner preparation—to tear the lettuce for the salad, or scrub the potatoes. Practical work which has visible results will help her to feel capable and will offer companionship with you at the same time. It may take extra effort on your part, but it is the best way to help her through this uncomfortable phase. Later, her capacity to play happily and creatively will return, at a more complex level, and she will occupy herself more harmoniously once again. It is important for children to go through this stage before they enter first grade; it helps prepare them for the new way of learning in grade school—for taking instruction from the loved teacher as an authority.

Second, we can also consider parental guilt and the role of entertainment. There is a need basic to human life: the need to feel needed and appreciated. While we would not wish to return to the era of child labor, I think the pendulum may have swung to the opposite extreme. Somehow the wish to preserve childhood—a worthy aim in one respect—has led to the feeling that we must ensure that everything is "fun." Add to this the subtle and not-so-subtle trends in society toward the you-can-have-it-all, instant gratification approach to life, which is constantly bombarding us from the media, and we arrive at an unfortunate situation in which children and young people grow up expecting that life owes them fun and entertainment. It is not difficult to observe manifestations of this syndrome, and it is a sad thing to contemplate how human creativity can be stifled and self-centered urges encouraged thereby.

Parents of young children can make a real contribution to society by countering this trend. In your own home life you can show by example that all family members contribute to the life of the household and consider the needs of others. Certainly there are times to play together, but there are also tasks that must be done in order to maintain the life of the family. Parents go to work, but they also have household work to be done: meals to prepare, the garden to be tended, floors to be scrubbed, laundry to be done, the car to be repaired or washed, and so forth. Children need to see "real life" being lived. They also need to experience that their help is needed, and required. Their contribution to family life will, of course, change according to age, but even a toddler can learn that Mommy needs to finish preparing dinner, or Daddy needs to finish washing the dishes. And even a toddler can "help" in more concrete ways, with the support and help of a parent. Gradually children can take on more responsibility for simple, regular chores. Of course this will at first require more work from the parents. It's often easier to do everything yourself. But consider that you are laying the foundation for a healthy family life, and teaching your child that she has a role to play in daily life.

If you constantly entertain your child, you will be giving her the false impression that the world exists for her pleasure and that she is without resources of her own. This is bound to cause difficulties later. A mother in our parent/child class expressed relief to see how happily and creatively her daughter had learned to play while the mother was involved in purposeful activity—ironing, mending, carding wool. She said, "I'd been feeling like a 'one-woman entertain-Susannah company.' I felt guilty if I had to stop playing with her to do the laundry or wash the dishes. Now I see how good it is for her to see me at work, and how well she plays."

Furthermore, boredom is a wonderful impetus to creativity and resourcefulness. If a child is always provided with activities and play ideas, she will not have a chance to be attuned to her own fantasy life, to play out her own inner world. This is a great loss, which will have later implications for her ability to think creatively and independently.

I would like to recommend a book which will inspire you to look at family life and the roles of parents and children. It is a series of musings on various aspects of life with young children, and is filled with thought-provoking ideas and practical suggestions for creating a life in harmony with basic human values. It contains much wisdom. The book, entitled *Mitten Strings for God: Reflections for Mothers in a Hurry*, is by Katrina Kenison, published by Warner Books. (The title should really be ". . . for Mothers and Fathers. . ." because fathers can learn a lot from it too!) It is a wonderfully inspiring, down-to-earth, humorous, poignant, and challenging book. 🌿

Telephone

Question

As soon as I start talking on the phone, my child seems to demand my attention. I find my attention split between her and the person on the phone. How can I handle this?

Answer

This situation requires some adjustment on both sides, but the first requirement is that you, the parent, be clear in your own mind about expectations and priorities. This is a balancing act between the reasonable needs of the child and those of the conversing adults. It seems that when a parent is on the phone, the child feels shut out, excluded. It is almost uncanny the way a child, happily occupied in another room, suddenly appears at your side, whiny and demanding, the minute a phone conversation begins.

I have occasionally tried to have a phone conversation with the parent of a young child, in which every other sentence is directed to the child. It might go like this: "My daughter says no one plays with her at school… No, it's not time for ice cream right now…Is there any way you could help her find some playmates?…Ice cream is for dessert…She mentions a little girl named Jane…Because ice cream is sweet and if you have it now it'll spoil your appetite…" And so on. No one is satisfied with a conversation like this.

It is important for children to learn to wait, and to respect others' needs, and it is the parent's responsibility to help the child develop these capacities. It is also important for the parent to be polite enough to consider the needs of the other person in the phone conversation. These are priorities on one side of the scale.

A helpful approach in this regard is to prepare for a phone call by checking to see that all is well with your child. Tell her, "Mommy/Daddy is going to make a phone call now. I'll check on you after I'm finished. Please don't interrupt while I'm on the phone." For a younger child, or one who tends to be clingy, you might set up something simple for the child near the phone (paper and crayons, a doll and blanket, or some other favorite play materials) and add, "If you want to be with Mommy/Daddy, you may play right here." This will take you only a moment, but will give the clear message that you are not trying to get away from your child: she is welcome to be with you, but will have her own activity while you are talking. One parent I know has a "telephone box" of special playthings which she takes out if she needs to be on the phone.

If your child does try to interrupt you, you can excuse yourself to the other person on the phone for a moment and tell your child gently but firmly, "Mommy/Daddy's job is to talk on the telephone; your job is to crayon (or whatever the child was doing). I'll talk to you when I'm fin-ished." Then resolutely ignore her attempts to interrupt. If she becomes too persistent, you might again excuse yourself and take her calmly to her room, paying no attention to her protests. When your phone call is over, give her a hug and a little extra attention for a moment. If you are firm and consistent in your expectations, she will learn to take phone calls bet-ter in stride.

If you are not initiating a phone call but are answering a call, you can ask the caller to wait a moment, if necessary, while you follow the above procedure, or something similar. Or, if it is a time when your child really needs you, ask the caller if you can call back in a few minutes. Your caller will probably prefer this to a conversation with many interruptions.

On the other side of the scale is the child's legitimate need to feel her parent's attention. As already mentioned, phone calls are truly difficult for many children, and it is asking too much of them if you spend a great deal of time on the phone. You show respect and consideration for your child's needs, and have a better chance of teaching her to respect your needs, if you try to limit your phone time to really necessary calls while she is up and about. Save longer calls or multiple calls for naptime or after she is in bed for the night (another good reason—in addition to your child's health—for an early bed time). Your child's cooperative spirit can shine best when it is not overtaxed, and if she learns through your consistent behavior that she needs to be patient while you are on the phone, but that phone calls do come to a timely end, this will go a long way toward balancing the needs of parent and child. 🌿

Bedtime Ritual

Question

My daughter's nighttime ritual usually includes the basics of getting ready for bed and a story or two. Then she snuggles down in bed and apprehensively awaits sleep to overcome her. Then, if she doesn't fall asleep in what she considers the appropriate amount of time, she gets very anxious, even distraught, and sleep will totally elude her. I wonder if perhaps reciting a verse or prayer would calm her and ease the transition to restful sleep. Do you have any insights into bedtime rituals, sleep anxieties, and verses to calm children?

Answer

It is frustrating for both parent and child when bedtime is a time of tension and anxiety. I have read somewhere that being able to fall asleep on his or her own is the infant's or young child's first step toward self-confidence and a sense of competence; so it is clearly worthwhile to support this process. Having a consistent, dependable ritual is the first step. It need not, and should not, be long and elaborate, but it should be followed unfailingly. It might begin with a bath; lavender oil in warm water can have a soothing, relaxing effect. You can "ritualize" even the smallest details, without making a big production of it—for example, wrapping her in a bath towel the same way, having her folded nightie ready in the same place, combing or brushing her hair, and so on, always in the same order. This kind of ritual imparts a deep sense of security to a young child, for whom actions always speak louder than words.

I recommend reading or telling only one story at bedtime, so she can really live with that story and not suffer from mental indigestion. We aim for quality, not quantity. Often when children beg for more stories, it is not so much the story content they crave as simply more time with the parent. Instead of an additional story, you might add to the ritual something that many children find very soothing and reassuring: a review of the day, a looking back at the child's or family's activities, beginning with the morning. This can be very simple, or more detailed, according to the child's age and inclinations, but it should be done as if one were looking at a picture scroll being unrolled—not discussing each experience but just recalling it.

The process should have a definite beginning, and a definite ending with the last event of the day. This can then be followed by a good-night song, if you wish (something simple, like "Twinkle, Twinkle Little Star," may be nice) and then a verse or prayer. It is best to choose one verse, memorize it, and use it regularly so that she becomes at home with it, rather than going from one to another. Some parents like to light a candle during the review, song, and verse. This adds a special mood of quiet and serenity. The candle is then snuffed out after the verse. Your child's teacher will be able to suggest appropriate verses for you to consider.

For a child who is struggling with anxieties, a way needs to be found to break the pattern of wakefulness. Two factors seem of great importance here: first, you should think through the bedtime ritual and decide how it should be carried out. You may want to add some new "security item" such as a beautiful new night light, or perhaps a sheepskin "lambie" to take to bed, or a soft bedtime doll. Second, you should cultivate an attitude of matter-of-fact confidence that your daughter is now ready to learn to fall asleep. Without discussing her previous difficulties, you can say something like, "Now you are cozy with your lambie, and you can lie here and think about [something pleasant that was mentioned in the day's review]. We'll see you in the morning." It may be best not even to mention falling asleep. If she expresses anxiety about it, tell her it's all right if she doesn't go to sleep till later, that it's all right just to rest in bed. You can say she will fall asleep when she's ready.

If she calls you later, you can give her a pat of reassurance, but do not linger or get into conversation, just reiterate that she's nice and cozy and you'll see her in the morning. Make sure there's a glass of water within reach, if she tends to ask for a drink. If she sees that you are not consumed with worry about the situation, this will go a long way to calming her.

One final thought: if none of the above seems to help after a few weeks have passed, you might look at what she eats for supper and experiment a little. It's possible that if she has a dessert with sugar, for example, this might cause wakefulness; or perhaps she has a food sensitivity that is disturbing her rest. If you suspect this might be a factor, you might keep track of her diet and see if you notice any patterns. This is something you wouldn't mention to her, but just try to notice yourself. ❧

Feeding a Child

Question

Our daughter often asks to be fed at mealtimes, complaining that she is tired. We are afraid that if we do not feed her, she will not get enough to eat. When she is at a friend's house, however, she eats by herself and people often comment on what a good eater she is. I realize that I actually enjoy feeding her; it seems to keep a close connection that was established in infancy. Is this something we should be concerned about?

Answer

Part of our task as parents is to support our children's healthy impulse to become competent, to learn to care for themselves, and ultimately to become self-directed, independent adults. This is a long process of parental "letting go," which really begins at birth. It is not always easy to discern how much independence is really age-appropriate; some children seem constantly to push against boundaries, especially at certain stages of development, while others have a tendency to be clingy or overly dependent, seemingly reluctant to move on to a new stage.

Feeding oneself is a basic life skill which begins to be practiced in infancy, starting of course with the sucking reflex, proceeding to learning to open the mouth when a spoonful of food approaches (we could call it the "baby bird" stage), progressing to self-feeding with finger foods, and finally to independent use of a spoon and, a little later, fork. Some children are neat, while others are messy, sometimes requiring a drop-cloth under the chair during the learning process. Whatever the child's particular style, he is developing competence and self-confidence through satisfying his hunger and experiencing the pleasure of different tastes and textures. He is also developing important social skills by learning to participate in meal times with the rest of the family.

Feeding a child who is capable of feeding himself diminishes the child's sense of self and of self-confidence. It may also be indulging the parent's pleasure in re-living an earlier period of the child's life, at the expense of the child's appropriate development. Unless a child is extremely ill, I would suggest it is best to expect the child to eat by himself and to find other, age-appropriate ways to satisfy the mutual need for intimacy between parent and child. If a child habitually complains of being too tired to eat, you can decide on a plan of action to attain your goal of supporting your child's developing self-confidence and independence rather than regression. For example, you could arrange for a short rest time before the meal, and have your child lie or play quietly in his room "to get ready for supper." Then at the meal time you could remind the child that he has already had his rest, and that now Mommy needs to eat her supper and he needs to eat his. If he insists on wanting to be fed, you can be firm about it and, when supper is over, just remove his plate and proceed with bedtime preparations. It will not take many times for him to get the message, if this is done in a calm and matter-of-fact way. Remember that your child will not starve, and don't get into the counterproductive pattern of letting him eat later. Once a pattern is established, you can eliminate the before-meal rest if it doesn't seem needed.

Another important practice in serving meals for young children is to give them very small helpings. It is better to give them a little at first and allow them to have second and even third helpings, than to overwhelm them with large portions. This cuts down on waste of food, which is an important value in itself, and is helpful, as well, when serving a new food or a food which the child does not like. You can have a policy that everyone has to take one bite of everything so they can "learn to like it." As a teacher, I found this a very beneficial approach, and many children were delighted and proud when they discovered that eventually they *had* learned to like a food.

Finally, a child who is asking to be fed may be looking for affirmation that he is indeed getting older and more capable, while indicating that he doesn't want to lose the sense of being cared for by the parent. It's important to satisfy both of these needs. You might say, "It's time for both of us to eat right now, but after we clear the table let's sit in the rocking chair and [feed your dolly] or [play the cobbler game]" or some other cozy activity. Your goal is to satisfy the child's need, without getting into an explanation, discussion, or argument. As in most child-rearing situations, actions speak louder than words. 🍂

Swords vs. Guns

Question

I notice that toy swords are available in the Little Shop, and that stories of Michael speak of swords. Why is it appropriate to use a sword as a toy, but not a gun?

Answer

This is a complicated question, and I don't have a clear, definitive answer. On the one hand, I'm not altogether comfortable with sword play; on the other hand, I have not always forbidden gun play under all circumstances, though at school I have never allowed children to point an imaginary gun at another person and I most often put away wood pieces that are being used as weapons. Almost every teacher I know has a slightly different approach to the "weapons issue," and I think each set of parents has to think this through for themselves. What I can do here is present some thoughts for your consideration.

Stories and legends of Michael, the heavenly being connected with courage and inner strength, portray his overcoming the dragon with a sword. Often this sword is described as a sword of light, or, in the story I told in the kindergarten, a heavenly sword, forged from the stars. In some stories, Michael does not actually slay the dragon, but "overcomes" it or even tames it. In every case, however, the confrontation between Michael and the dragon is a picture of the struggle within each of us between our higher self and our lower self—a struggle in which we all have need of strength and courage. Children who hear the story of Michael will feel a sense of respect for his heavenly sword, and possessing a sword may bring a feeling of Michael's influence. I have heard some teachers describe the making of wooden swords in the classroom, to be used at circle time, as a profound and satisfying project for the children during the Michaelmas season in the fall.

It may be helpful to reflect on the difference between a sword and a gun. Both can injure or kill. To use swords, however, requires that the combatants be in direct contact, within physical reach of each other. They must, in a sense, "know" each other and therefore take responsibility for their deeds. The use of a gun, however, has at least the possibility of being more impersonal and thus, in a way, amoral (if not immoral). Swords are non-technological; the opposite extreme, one might say, are modern "smart" missiles. When these are used, the attacker is nowhere near the potential victim. It is not that I am in favor of solving problems by the sword; I am just sharing reflections on what seems to me a qualitative difference between swords and guns, a difference involving the level of consciousness and sense of responsibility of the user.

It is a fairly widely-observed fact that many children, especially boys, seem to have an inborn urge toward gun play, no matter how peace-loving their parents may be or how the parents may try to shield them from exposure to weapons. The reasons for this urge may be debated, but the fact is pretty clear. The issue for every parent and every teacher is how to respond to this urge. I found with some groups of children that if I tried absolute prohibition of weapons, the result was deceptiveness: "This is a flashlight!" (accompanied by a guilty look). I felt that duplicity was not a quality I wanted to encourage. The "forbidden fruit" syndrome could also take hold.

Rules I felt comfortable with were: a) no aiming or pointing at people; b) no realistic toy guns—children would have to use their imagination; c) if using swords, no actual striking of other people. With younger children, no reason for these rules need be given, and if there is a problem, removing the "weapon" and bringing the child to another activity is the best approach. As in other matters with the younger ones, actions speak louder than words. With older children (age five to seven, perhaps), the adult may say quietly but firmly, "I don't like you to point guns at people, because guns can hurt people." It is sometimes good that they hear your moral position, though without lecturing or preaching. On the other hand, it is important not to give children the sense that everyone who uses a gun is "bad;" after all, guns are used in law enforcement, and some people hunt for food. This is one of those issues where it may be necessary to establish, "This is how we do it in our family," or "This is how it is at school," tacitly acknowledging that others may have a different approach. ❧

TV Away from Home

Question

Our children don't watch television or videos at home, but if they see it at another house—when we're visiting relatives, for example—it makes such an impression that their play and conversation are affected for a long time. How can we help them get this out of their system? Also, what can we do about the fact that our children sometimes stay with a neighbor who lets her children watch television regularly? I don't feel I can ask her to turn off their TV.

Answer

It is of course difficult, if not impossible, to control children's exposure to electronic media when you are away from home. To a certain extent you can avoid places where you know the television will be a presence; for example, you can plan a picnic or other outing as a way of getting together with friends who are likely to have the TV on at home. But this sort of avoidance is not always feasible. And spending time with relatives is important for children, even if they watch TV!

To address the second part of the question first: I see that it could seem presumptuous and judgmental to ask someone to turn off the TV when your children are there, and if it is a situation where you need care for your children and you have no other options, it is particularly difficult. If it is simply a case of playmates, you can encourage playing outdoors or at your house as much as possible, as one approach. Otherwise, I think it is possible at least to let the relatives or neighbors know that you avoid having the TV on when your children are playing. One parent found it was helpful to say, "My child seems to do better if she doesn't watch TV." You could follow by mentioning what effects you have observed from TV-watching. In this way, you are not judging what they do, or preaching the evils of television, but simply sharing an observation with them out of your experience. Beyond that, I think you can only do what's possible in your situation, and realize that your home environment and all that you offer your children are helping to balance out their experiences and mitigating the effects of any TV they may see. It is also important to maintain an attitude of warmth and respect for the other people as human beings, so your children do not experience a sense of discord.

Regarding the sometimes long-term effects of what a child actually sees on television:

Children need to "play out" what they experience, and sometimes "talk it out" as well. We can accept this need, as it applies to television influences, without condemning it; but we need not get caught up in the play ourselves or encourage and prolong it, for example by supplying the children with costumes, accessories, or toys on the TV theme. If the children create their own outfits and accessories, at least they are exercising their creative imagination! This is a question which could call forth a long answer, and of course every child and every situation is unique. To be more brief, however, I would say it is best to watch or listen to your children in an accepting, yet neutral, way, and watch for opportunities to lead them on to some other activity. I have found it is often good to say, in response to a child's telling about something he saw on TV, "Thank you for telling me; now let's eat our snack" (or whatever is happening at the time). This seems to satisfy the child that he has been heard and acknowledged, but it leads him on to something in the "here and now."

We certainly don't want children to feel that we disapprove of them because they saw something on television. Our goal, rather, would be to offer them plenty of experiences to counterbalance the effects of the television images: music, stories and puppetry, active play, artistic activities, and perhaps most important of all, experiences of the world of nature and its rhythms. These experiences will strengthen your children so that they are able to move forward in a healthy way.

Barbie

Question

My daughter is persistent in asking me to buy her a Barbie doll; some of her friends have them and she sees them sometimes when we are at the store. She says, "Why can't we just buy one?!" I feel she is so young to have a doll like that, and Barbie is not a role model I want for her. I had one when I was eight or ten, but by then I was able to take care of it, dressing it and arranging its hair. When I see little girls carrying a Barbie doll around, it is usually a mess, hair disarranged, no clothes on. . . I have been telling her she can have one when she is eight, but this does not satisfy her. What else can I say to her?

Answer

I agree that a Barbie doll is not an appropriate doll for a young child. As you say, young children are not really able to dress and groom them, and the dolls offer a role model of pseudo-sexiness and external glamour that is not particularly nourishing to a little child who is very much in the process of taking in—internalizing through example—what it is to be a human being.

What bothers me the most about Barbie dolls is that they are dishonest, or perhaps deceptive is a better word, in a rather subtle but very basic way. In the first place, although they appear to be "realistic," their proportions are actually not quite right. More disturbing, though, is the fact that they look soft and curvy, but they feel hard and lifeless. In this sense, they are ugly while being made to appear beautiful.

Your question, however, is what to say to your daughter. This question I must answer in the same way I would answer whether it concerned a Barbie doll, watching TV, staying up late, eating ice cream just before dinner, or anything you feel is not suitable for your child. Unfortunately there is really no way to convince your child not to want something! A young child is developmentally simply unable to use rational thinking to overcome strong will impulses. Your child needs you to provide her with boundaries until she is older and can gradually take over this function.

The best thing you can do is to be as sure as you can be that you are acting in your child's best interests. Then be patient, firm, and consistent. Realize that your daughter doesn't have to like the position you are taking—that indeed, she can't really be expected to—but that you are being a good parent by making a decision that is healthy for her. This realization will help you to be firm without getting angry.

In the case of the wish for a Barbie doll, it might be worth considering whether providing a more appropriate doll with a variety of doll clothes would be helpful. Perhaps she already has this; but if not, and if you should decide to give her one, you should avoid offering it explicitly as a substitute for Barbie. It is a very good thing for a child to learn to dress and undress a doll; it is an excellent way to develop dexterity and eye-hand coordination. A five-year-old (or older) child would even benefit from helping to stitch very simple clothes or blankets for a doll, as long as this is done without pressure or expectations on the part of the parent. With a basket of fabric scraps and trim, some children might really enjoy creating all sorts of outfits.

Essentially, though, you will just have to stick to your decision, as you have been doing. Sometimes there doesn't seem to be an easy answer.

Forbidden Words?

Question

Do you recommend making words such as stupid and hate "no" words in our house? I've heard different theories for and against.

Answer

As I'm sure you've heard us say many times, it is always best to be positive—to tell children what to do rather than what not to do. Certainly there are times when we must say "no" in a very direct way, and there are a few words that I would forbid. These are words, like the "f-word," for example, that a child may have picked up somewhere, perhaps not knowing the meaning but sensing that their use can cause delightful shock in the parents. In such cases it is good to say, firmly but matter-of-factly, "We don't say [whatever the word is] at our house." You might say, if questioned, "It's not polite." Hearing you say the word yourself removes much of the shock value. I have used this technique successfully as a teacher.

I don't think it's a good idea, though, to have many words covered by such a rule. It may be helpful to think about why you don't like the words "stupid" and "hate." Sometimes thinking of the principle can help you find a way to handle the situation. To me, the word "stupid" is demeaning, whether applied to a person, an idea, or an object. Rather than forbid the word, which really wouldn't teach the child anything, I might say instead, "His name is Billy. We don't call people names." Or, "If you don't like spinach, you may say, 'I don't care for spinach.' " In the first case, we are teaching respect for other people; in the second, we are helping a child learn to express himself more appropriately and, actually, more precisely. Still another example: If you said, "I like this picture," and your child responded, "It's stupid!" you might say, "People can like different things. It's all right if you don't like it." Of course every case will be slightly different, but perhaps these examples can give you an idea of how, without denying the child's reaction, you can gradually help him learn better ways to express himself.

The word "hate" is more difficult; it really has the power to wound, especially if directed at a person, and often there is great anger involved when it is spoken. Forbidding the word, however, does not address the anger and frustration. Again, I think it's better to let the child know what to say, for example: "You can tell me you're angry;" or, "You're really angry; you can tell me about it after you've calmed down." If you do feel you wish to forbid the word "hate," you could say, "You can tell me you're angry, but we don't say 'I hate you' in our family."

Forbidding too many words is, in a sense, an admission of weakness; it says that you are unable to cope with them. You want, rather, to show your child the capacity to overcome impulses and strive to be an upright human being. What is important for your child, I feel, is to perceive that you are not shocked or frightened by his use of words. He needs to experience your calm, firm direction which will help him learn how to express, and thus cope with, strong reactions. If you leave him without boundaries or guidance, he will be confused and fearful. He will thrive in the presence of a strong, loving adult whose inner firmness provides a model for imitation.

Appropriate Gifts

Question

My son has many generous friends and relatives. What suggestions do you have for guiding them toward appropriate gifts to give him on special occasions? I've tried describing the school, the philosophy, and gift ideas. Somehow people don't understand or know where to shop. They really want to give.

Answer

This is a delicate matter which requires tact and a certain amount of flexibility on the part of parents. Some friends and relatives may be amenable to suggestions, particularly if these are presented in the spirit of wanting to help them choose gifts which will be most enjoyed by your child. A positive statement may be helpful, such as, "Our child seems to play best with toys which don't make noises. He is good at supplying his own sound effects, and mechanical ones seem to make him over-excited." Or you might say, "Our son is at a stage when he really loves to imitate workmen. A hard hat or a trowel and bucket or a tool belt would make a great gift." You could also suggest sources for shopping or for ordering toys which you think are appropriate, or even provide a catalog or two.

Even so, some people will not want to follow your suggestions. They may honestly feel your child will be deprived if he does not have the latest in talking dolls or battery-operated vehicles. In such a case, it is best to accept the gift graciously for the sake of your child and family (or friendly) relationships. After all, the gift has been given in love, and you do not want your child to feel guilty for receiving the gift, or to feel that you disapprove of someone important to him.

Some parents report that after some time has passed and the novelty has worn off, they are able to put these gifts away, out of sight. It may be a good opportunity, in fact, to sort through your child's toys and gather up those which are not used often or are not in good condition any more. In this way you are not singling out the "undesirable" toy. If asked, you can say the toys are resting. This is an expression we sometimes use at school and it seems to make sense to the children.

In any case, where toys are concerned, "Less is more." Too many toys are distracting to children and may actually interfere with their ability to focus their play. It is far better to have fewer playthings and take good care of them. A periodic clearing out is a fine thing. You could also consider rotating the playthings, or bringing out one that has been resting for a while for an occasion when a change is needed. A child who generally plays in a healthy way with materials which nurture him will surely not be deeply harmed by a toy you might rather he did not have. Out of his capacity for fantasy play, he will probably be able to transform and redeem the quality of the toy. 🌿

"What did you learn in school today?"

Question

People keep asking my daughter, "So, what did you learn in school today?" She replies, "Nothing!" Lately she is coming to me, wondering why it is that she does not learn anything in her school. I try to explain that she learns new things every day—for example, she learns how to make bread, and many other wonderful things, from her teachers. But this answer does not seem to satisfy her. What should I say?

Answer

It sounds as if both the questioners and your daughter are assuming that "learning" means something academic; perhaps she has picked up that idea from the manner or context of the questions. It is probably not possible to help a child of this age to understand the deeper meaning and significance of learning, so it is best to forego explanations.

There are, however, some other things you might do. First of all, if the adults asking the question are people you see frequently, it would be a good idea to take the time, when your daughter is not present, to tell them briefly about her school and the philosophy. Of course it would be best if they didn't ask her for a report about school, but if they can't resist, you could suggest they just ask, for example, what she did at school, or whether she played with her friends, etc.

When your daughter asks you why she isn't learning anything in her school, you can tell her in a confident tone, without going into detail, that she is learning just what she needs to learn right now. If she presses further, you can say, "Are you wondering when you will learn to read and write? You will begin to learn those things when you go to first grade next year. That's how it works in our school." With this question, just as when Acorn Hill six-year-olds are asked by friends or neighbors why they aren't in first grade, children simply need to be reassured by their parents that they are just where they need to be right now. "This is how we are doing it" is a concept that applies to many family practices, whether it is holding back on academics, keeping the TV off, following a vegetarian diet, or any other practice that may be different from some friends or neighbors.

Finally, you can try, as a parent, to take such question-and-answer situations lightly, and not to feel somehow defensive on behalf of your daughter. Depending on the particular nature of the conversation, you might just smile at your daughter's answer of "nothing" and go on your way with her. If, however, she seems uncomfortable or at a loss, you might suggest to her in a matter-of-fact way, "You could tell Mr. Jones that this was painting day." You don't really owe Mr. Jones any more than that, although you could, if it seemed necessary, add the remark to Mr. Jones that your daughter will be going to first grade next year. This would give the message to your daughter that first grade is the time for "learning" as she currently understands it.

In summary, a confident, matter-of-fact attitude on your part will help more than any explanations to make your daughter comfortable with her school experience. Remember that it is a good thing for children to aspire to something they will be able to do when they are older. It will fill them with a sense of wonder and anticipation when they finally are ready to begin their grade school years. As the parent of a new first grader told me joyfully, "Last year she wasn't ready for first grade. This year, after another year of kindergarten, she is just SO READY to be there!"

Toys in the Neighborhood

Question

Concerning toys, we would like to create a home environment in harmony with what our child has at Acorn Hill. Other children in the neighborhood, however, like to play with plastic toys and video games, and friends and relatives give our child those kinds of toys. As a consequence, she has many "non-Waldorf" toys, and we feel uncomfortable about this. How can we manage this situation?

Answer

This is a situation which confronts many Waldorf families, not only in the area of toys, but in other aspects of lifestyle as well. In fact, it is often a set of values different from mainstream culture which draws families to Waldorf education. It then becomes an issue of creating a family way of life congruent with your values without alienating yourselves from neighbors, friends, and relatives. There is no simple, once-and-for-all solution to this issue; the mutual support of like-minded families is often the most help.

In response to the specific question about toys, I would like to suggest several points for consideration.

Less is more! This applies to "Waldorf toys" as well as non-Waldorf play materials. Having a few well-chosen playthings encourages creativity, initiative, and the sense of gratitude and appreciation. It also makes the daily clean-up less overwhelming. Too many toys can undermine the capacity to focus, because of the distraction of so many items lying around. If you find yourself in the situation of too many toys—overflowing your storage capacity, strewn all over the house, or many items which your child doesn't really use—you could simply get rid of the excess, perhaps giving them to a charitable organization. Or, you can rotate toys, putting some away for a period of time, then getting them out and putting others away, rather like a museum's rotating exhibits.

If friends or relatives give your child toys which you would rather he/she not have, this can create a delicate situation. It is good to remember not to become dogmatic, and to realize that a toy given with love is, in a certain way, redeemed, and can be transformed by your child's love in return. It is important for your child to experience your love for the gift-giver, rather than your disapproval of the gift, which the child cannot be expected to understand. You can receive the gift graciously and let your child play with it for a period of time. Later, when the novelty has worn off, you can put it away. At school, when we have to put a plaything away (for example, if it is being misused), we say it is "resting." This seems to make sense to the children. It is best not to talk to your child about the quality of the toy, trying to explain or persuade why you find a toy undesirable. This is a concern which is the adult's responsibility, not the child's.

Some friends and relatives are amenable to gift suggestions; others, however, are not. It is important to be sensitive to such situations. I would probably, however, draw the line at video games or computer games for pre-schoolers, since there is growing evidence that these are really harmful for young children. To people open to suggestion, you can provide information about possible sources for good quality toys. Such toys, however, can be quite expensive, and it is helpful to be aware that "real" things can also be greatly enjoyed by children—muffin tins or a mason's trowel for sand play, a hammer and some scrap lumber, child-size work gloves, some bulbs to be planted, some squares of fabric, a baseball cap. . .

Neighborhood children will probably get used to the style of your child's playthings, and may even enjoy the novelty. You can help them enjoy your home by occasionally offering some special activity such as baking rolls or cookies, or providing supplies for simple craft projects. You could also try "priming the pump" by helping them get started in play, for example creating a house by draping sheets or blankets over chairs.

A creative child can use any play equipment imaginatively. Our goal, however, is to encourage and support this capacity for imaginative fantasy play, and later for problem-solving and goal-oriented activity, by providing materials which are open-ended, drawing out and exercising the child's inner capacities. Our own inner capacities as parents and teachers are challenged by the need to pursue this goal without creating an atmosphere of negativity and isolation around our children. 🌿

The following is an article written in response to the sudden death of a parent in our school.

Helping Children in a Time of Trouble—A Few Thoughts

In a time of trouble, such as the death of a family member or friend, parents are faced with the question of how to help their children through this time. In a sense, the question will have as many answers as there are particular children, since children respond so differently to a situation according to their age and nature. Parents are frequently brought up short by the realization that they must first face their own feelings and questions. Next comes the necessity of dealing with a child's questions.

A generally accepted "rule of thumb" in responding to children's questions is to give only as much information as the child is actually requesting. As adults, our thoughts on a topic tend to be quite far-ranging, while the child's question is likely to be on a much more direct level. It is better to err on the side of simplicity; if a child needs to know more, another question will surely follow. Your answer to "What happens to someone who has died?" will, of course, depend on your own view of this; in any case, a simple picture is usually best for a child. Your honest expression of sorrow and sympathy is very beneficial in helping a child to experience and cope with loss, but uncontrolled emotions are usually troubling or even frightening for the young child. The adult's effort to recognize and accept grief without being overwhelmed by it can be a profound example to a child.

Some children may appear to become obsessed by the death, asking question after question and seeming unsatisfied by any number of answers. The sensitive parent will soon realize that this child is seeking something other than words to quiet his or her anxieties. Often the best answer is a warm hug and words such as, "That's enough talk for now; come, it's time to pick some flowers for the supper table" (or some other such homely task). This child needs most of all an expression of love from the parent and the reassurance that life will go on, in the form of normal activities, even in the midst of grief. This is not to deny the grief, but to help the child to work through it in the way most natural to children: through activity. If it seems appropriate, the child can be encouraged to help bake a loaf of bread for the bereaved family, or perhaps to make a card to send.

The place of ritual in helping children and adults to cope with loss should not be overlooked. Rituals are "special times for special happenings," in the words of Julius Segal, a psychologist writing in the *Washington Post* some years ago. Such rituals, which may be religious, secular, or familial in origin, "can provide a strengthening sense of order and meaning in times of trouble. They can help maintain the form and rhythm of lives shaken by trauma and grief. . ." For a child who shows a continuing, deep concern about a death, establishing a simple ritual can be very comforting. For example, the child may help to create a special setting with perhaps a candle, a small vase of flowers, some beautiful autumn leaves, some acorns or crystals. . . and at a particular time each day (just before or after dinner, possibly, or before the bedtime story) the candle may be lighted and a song may be sung, or a verse recited, "to send our thoughts" or "to send our love" to the one who has died or to the family. Such a ritual may serve as a kind of anchor in a sea of grief or anxiety, as well as diminish the sense of helplessness in the face of another's loss.

Finally, a story which contains a simple but meaningful picture of the spiritual origins of life and its destinies can be of great help to a child. From such a story—as from all true stories—the child can take the image or images which will be of most help to him or her.

Is the World a Good Place?

Question

How can we understand Rudolf Steiner's statement that young children should experience that the world is good? Even in his day, the world was a troubled place, and it is surely even more dangerous today.

Answer

From time to time, local or global events cause fear and anxiety. As we live through uncertain times, we parents and teachers can experience a great blessing in our time spent with young children. Watching them at work and play, and observing their shining faces—alight with glee at one moment, crumpling in despair at another—we realize how completely they live in the present moment, and with what total devotion they give themselves over to all that they do.

Rudolf Steiner did say that children in their first seven years need to experience that the world is good. What can he have meant, considering that in his day, just us in ours, there is clearly a great deal in the world that is not good? How often a child falls down and gets hurt! How he suffers with illness and fever! How she protests when Mommy and Daddy leave her with a babysitter! Perhaps the elderly man next door suffers a heart attack and dies. And, as the media constantly remind us, danger and violent acts may threaten us. How, then, can we expect a child to experience the world as good? If we tried to present such a picture of the world, wouldn't we be lying to our child? And why, since the world is in fact full of trouble and danger, would we nevertheless want a child to think it is good?

Each of us may have a different response to the statement, "The world is good." One person may feel it is only true to say, "There is goodness in the world," a more limited statement. Another may have a world view which supports the idea that the cosmic order is "good" in the sense that every occurrence and every living thing has a necessary role to play in world evolution, even though we may not always understand the necessity. Such existential issues are worth pondering. Here I would like to offer just a few thoughts for your consideration. You can fill them out with your own reflections; and you may come up with other answers, of course.

I believe it *is* important for the child to experience the world as good. Such experience supports the child's natural trust and unconscious confidence that he can grow and learn and find his way into the future. It is this trust and confidence that gives the child the courage throughout life to meet and overcome the challenges which will surely come. These challenges, which may at first seem to be "bad" experiences, are in fact opportunities for growth. The individual who can approach them with trust and confidence will be well-equipped to summon the inner resources necessary to benefit from such opportunities.

Consider the little child's world. To an infant lying in Mother's or Daddy's arms, the whole world seems to exist in the parent's eyes, and this world is indeed good. As the infant grows and begins to sit up and then to crawl and finally walk, the world expands to the larger circle of home and family, and then to extended family and close friends. A home in which the child has a secure place, where there is a measure of attention to beauty and order, where there is a healthy rhythm, conveys to the child that the world is good. When a child suffers an injury or illness, the comfort offered by a calm and loving adult restores the sense of goodness.

It is, in fact, through the mediation of the adult that a little child experiences the world, in the sense that our attitudes and our moral bearing, as well as our actions, work deeply on the child. The child's world consists—and should consist—of what is in the immediate surroundings. This places a great responsibility on us. Rudolf Steiner's words, and the realization that we are the little child's world, can guide us in the present world situation. When we are with our children, we can try to set aside our concerns about our adult world, and do our best to be fully present in our daily activities. Mental health experts recommend that adults try to maintain normal routines and activities in times of stress. This is wise advice, and it applies to our children's world most strongly. We need to keep their familiar routines intact.

We should also be mindful of the old saying, "Little pitchers have big ears." Children have an uncanny ability to take in what adults are saying, even when they seem not to be listening. Even if they cannot possibly understand the content of what they are hearing, they are absorbing the feelings and underlying meaning, and they will be affected. Being exposed to adult fears can seriously undermine a child's ability to experience the world as good. We need to find the strength to save anxious conversation for times when the children are not present.

Of course when a sad or frightening experience does occur in the child's small world, it must be dealt with rather than denied, so that the child may be comforted and may share in the healing and recovery of goodness as the adults meet and cope with the situation. The important thing, once again, is to keep in mind the child's natural capacity for living in the present, in the immediate experience. Let us not ask our children to share our adult concerns and our consciousness of the larger world. Let us rather help them to experience the world as good, so that they—the future of our world—may grow in trust and confidence and strength.

In Conclusion...

When I was a young parent, I once complained to a respected mentor, "I wish I were older and wiser so I could be a better parent." "Well, just think," she responded, "if you were older you wouldn't have nearly as much energy." Our children demand the best we have to offer, and many times that "best" does not seem good enough. We can easily become discouraged and frustrated; we may feel we are failing our children, whom we love so much. Since meeting Waldorf education and the work of Rudolf Steiner, I have had many reasons to feel grateful, both as a parent and as a teacher. Of particular help and inspiration has been an insight he offered in various contexts and which I would like to share here as I understand it: in living and working with children, it is not perfection we need. Rather, it is our striving to become better, to develop our capacities, that really nourishes those in our care.

It seems to me the very idea of "perfection" can convey a sense of coldness, of rigidity, of fixedness. Striving, however, brings warmth and movement, which can encourage our children and provide a wonderful example of the essence of what it is to be a human being: the capacity to grow and change, to learn, to exert ourselves for the sake of others. Such honest, consistent striving is, I believe, one of the greatest gifts we can offer our children. Of course our children, too, are constantly growing and learning—so it seems we will never catch up! May you enjoy the journey. Nothing can be more worthwhile.

About the Author

Nancy Foster has been a Waldorf kindergarten teacher since 1973 at Acorn Hill Waldorf Kindergarten and Nursery in Silver Spring, Maryland, where she now works with parents and children in parent/child groups. She also lectures, offers workshops for teachers at Waldorf kindergarten conferences, serves as a mentor for new teachers, and is on the visiting faculty of Sunbridge College in Spring Valley, New York. She is the author/editor of two collections of seasonal music and verse, *Let Us Form a Ring* and *Dancing as We Sing*. She and her husband, a professional musician, encountered Waldorf education and Anthroposophy while seeking a school for their two sons, now grown.